iPhone 11 Pro and Pro Max Camera Users Guide

Smartphone Digital Photography from Learner to Advance in taking photos like a Pro and an Expert

Wendy Hills

You are welcome to join the Fan's Corner, here

iPhone 11 Pro and Pro Max Camera Users Guide

Smartphone Digital Photography Manual from Learner to Advance in taking photos like a Pro and an Expert

Wendy Hills

Disclaimer

The advice and strategies found within may not be suitable for every situation. This work is sold with the understanding that neither the author nor the publisher is held responsible for the results accrued from the advice in this book.

Prologue

Hey, you have got the iPhone 11 Pro and Pro Max and want to maximize the use of its many camera lenses, then congratulations on your purchasing this **iPhone 11 Pro and Pro Max Camera Users Guide.** This book is a comprehensive guide for anyone who wants to deploy his or her iPhone 11 Pro to immediately start snapping amazing photos.

With this book, your eyes will be opened to the many basic and advanced functions that the iPhone 11 Pro and Pro Max camera comes with, which can be utilized towards creating amazing pictures at a professional level with only your phone.

For users of older versions of the iPhone and are yet to still find their way around the iPhone 11 Pro and Pro Max and are having difficulties locating some of their favorite functions, then you will need this book to show you around as a real estate agent would show you round a new apartment till you master your way around the place.

Very often, the manuals that are shipped with our devices tend not to be poorly done and do not attempt to do enough in making it easy to start using such devices, in some other instances, they can be over technical and written with too many assumptions of the user's knowledge on the subject. Many other "Getting Started Guides" are sometimes too thin and do not really solve any problem, which is why this book is a real gem.

This book will immediately get you started on the most effective ways of using the iPhone 11 Pro and Pro Max to start taking amazing pictures by ensuring you get to better know the mobile phone you carry around and how you can also use them as your photography device whenever you go on a trip, attend an event, visit a location, or casting a scene.

Ensuring you get to know how to get the most from this digital camera in your pocket is what this book is about, after all, after spending so much to get your iPhone 11 Pro, you naturally would want to get more out of it.

With this book, you will learn how to use the camera on your iPhone 11 Pro better and be better able to optimize the camera features in a lot more ways than you have ever imagined.

As you start exploring the pages of this book, you will become exposed to a broad range of fantastic photographic and video tools that you had probably taken for granted or completely overlooked to a position where you now know how to use them.

For those who order this book, this book can help you get better on your use of your iPhone camera, especially for those the things you were not aware it could do. You soon will find out as others have done that this book is quite worth the time and money spent on it and highly recommended to anyone who uses their iPhone 11 Pro and Pro Max to take pictures.

With this book, you can now start using your iPhone 11 Pro camera and in taking the kind of photos that nobody will even believe were shot by you with an iPhone or by you.

Expected Contents

How to Use this Book

This book is written to serve as a guide to using the iPhone 11 Pro and Pro Max Camera, it is however not meant to replace the manufacturer's user guide, rather, it aims to compliment that guide in an easy to understand way.

The content of this book is written with the intention for it to be arranged in the best logical order from what the author considers to be from the elementary aspect of using the camera to more advanced stuff.

Although this approach has been found from experience to be most effective, however, each section is also strong enough to stand on its own, such that you can jump right in to any part of the book that you feel will be more useful to you at any point.

Introduction

The iPhone 11 Pro series is the most appealing iPhone Apple has ever made, and it comes with lovely designs and friendly sizes. It has a triple-lens rear camera to take photos and videos from a variety of perspectives, a new night mode to enhance low-light photography and extra battery life span, with battery lasting up to 18hours. The iPhone 11 comes packed with significant modifications in terms of camera and battery upgrade iPhone users have been desiring.

The iPhone 11 family comes with screen sizes of 5.8-inch, 6.5-inch, and 6.1-inch depending on if the phone is the iPhone 11, Pro, or Pro Max. They are an advanced version of the iPhone, which can sometimes make it a little difficult for new users or users of previous versions to hit the ground running, especially when they want to use their camera, yet the learning curve doesn't have to be steep, and it can become easy to use with the help of a guide like this.

The iPhone 11 comes with an IPS LCD screen of 326ppi and a topnotch Face ID tech, the selfie snapper, and the top speaker. The iPhone 11 also boasts of Apple's new A13 Bionic processor that emphasizes machine learning. Apple affirms that it's both the fastest CPU and GPU in a smartphone, with an advanced neural engine, machine learning accelerators, and Core ML3, all of these add up to an incredibly powerful chip that makes the phone operates faster and ensuring that everyone who uses the iPhone 11 Pro or Pro Max can enjoy the best of user experience.

The iPhone 11 uses Apple's Face ID TrueDepth camera with its updated 7MP for its front camera. All models of the iPhone 11 are fitted with 12MP, f/2.2 aperture camera, and Apple has introduced a brand-new selfie feature for capturing your selfie videos at 120 fps. Also, very little modification was done to the Apple ducts in terms of bezels by retaining the bezels as on its successor to the iPhone XR, as you would expect the design is still a tremendous improvement over phones like the iPhone 8, but the front of the iPhone 11 Pro remained unchanged. It has with it a thick and uniform bezel surrounding the 6.5-inch screen, and there is a similar wide notch at the top, having the TrueDepth camera and sensors for Face ID. The iPhone 11 Pro has far more features when compared to the bezel-less screen of the OnePlus 7, or the Galaxy Note 10 with its hole-punch camera.

The rear camera system is where Apple truly differentiates between iPhone 11 Pro and 11. Apple introduced a new triple-camera system on the iPhone 11 Pro models, whereas it was contented to put a dual-camera lens on the iPhone 11, which is still highly efficient in taking quality images. The features of the iPhone 11 Pro and Pro Max camera include:

Camera 1: 12 Mega Pixel wide cam, distance with Aperture of f/1.8

Camera 2: 12 Mega Pixel telephoto long-range lens, Aperture f/2.0, OIS, 2x optical zoom in and out.

Camera 3: 12 Mega Pixel ultra-wide camera, f/2.4, 120-degree FOV

The triple-camera system in the iPhone 11 Pro and Pro Max is more than just an extra lens, and Apple declares that's her engineers precisely calibrated each camera individually for things like white balance and exposure.

They pushed it even further by combining the three cameras and calibrating them for module synchronization gain. There is also the introduction of a new Night Mode for taking useable shots in extremely low light; then, there is the portrait mode and portrait lighting, next-generation Smart HDR, and advanced red-eye correction and auto image stabilization. And the iPhone 11 Pro and Pro Max can snap both wide and ultra-wide images simultaneously.

As far as video is concerned, iPhone 11 Pro and Pro Max record in 4K at up to 60fps, and features audio zoom (which focuses the microphone on your subject as you zoom), brighter True Tone flash, and the new QuickTake video that lets you use the shutter to change to video mode quickly.

The iPhone 11 can be used for up to 4 hours than the iPhone XS, similarly, the iPhone 11 Pro can be used over 18 hours more, while the iPhone 11 Max can be up to almost 20 hours. As far as charging is concerned, iPhone 11 has on-board wireless charging and fast charging via a 12W or higher power adapter, however, the iPhone 11 includes an 18W charger in the box. With a battery capacity of 3,110mAh, support for 18W charging, and support for water protection this phone is arguably one of the best phones in the market that you can own, which by reading this guide, you can be more proficient in using.

In terms of the phone's water protection, the iPhone 11 is rated for high IP68 water resistance, which means it can be dunked in 2 meters of water (6.5 feet) for up to 30 minutes without facing any damage. The iPhone 11 with enough storage space starts from 64 GB to 256 GB to 512 GB for you to be able to save your photos after taking them and comes with a flash cable and a pair of EarPods that ends on a flash connector. It is checked with a durable glass made by Corning, which is a custom Gorilla Glass with a slight 2.5D finish around the bottom. The front glass has an oleophobic (oil repellent) coating, which makes it more difficult for fingerprints to stick to it and easier to clean when they do.

The iPhone 11 has an aluminum frame with a brushed finish and the usual left side silent switch and volume buttons, the control key and the right SIM tray, and the bottom lightning port with the second speaker and mouthpiece. The photos tab in the Photos app has four different views on the iPhone 11 that include Years, Months, Days, and All Photos. This is a feature adopted by the iOS 13. The Days, Months, and Years tabs use what the Artificial Intelligence (AI) considers as best pictures at a glance, which helps to have the clutter filtered and prevents screenshots, notes and some other categories from showing and when you scroll through your photos in these categories, live pictures and videos will play automatically, though muted and all your best photos or videos will appear in larger thumbnails.

The iPhone 11 offers spatial audio, a 3D sound model made possible by a new sound visualizer, which provides support for Dolby Atmos, which helps to make each audio sound sharper, louder, and more impressive on all new iPhones. With two small speakers, the difference in quality won't be Home Pod quality or anything, but you can expect it to be optimized sound quality and an improved one. The iPhone 11 Pro and Pro Max are

Apple's latest flagship mostly because of its extra zoom lens, slightly better battery life, and high resolutions.

The Pro Max's camera isn't that different from the iPhone 11 Pro even though the Apple iPhone 11 Max is one of the largest luxury smartphones with a 6.5-inch screen Super Retina XDR OLED display, an A13 Bionic chipset which is Apple's latest, and up to 512 GB of internal storage. Just like the iPhone 11 Pro, it comes with three multipurpose cameras that can perform different functions, cameras that include both the primary wide-angle and the telephoto camera, which both offers the same focal length the predecessor XS Max had and also an ultra-wide camera with a focus and an equivalent 13mm field of view.

On the image sensing side of things, the new Deep Fusion technology uses the chipset's neural engine and advanced machine learning to perform pixel-by-pixel optimization for better textures, lower noise, and a wider dynamic. The iPhone 11 Max's new imaging features alongside its redesigned camera interface, seamless zooming in the video, live bokeh, and HDR preview all combine to make the use of the iPhone 11 Pro and Pro Max phones for taking still photos and shooting videos and films a great experience.

Chapter 1

Smartphone Photography

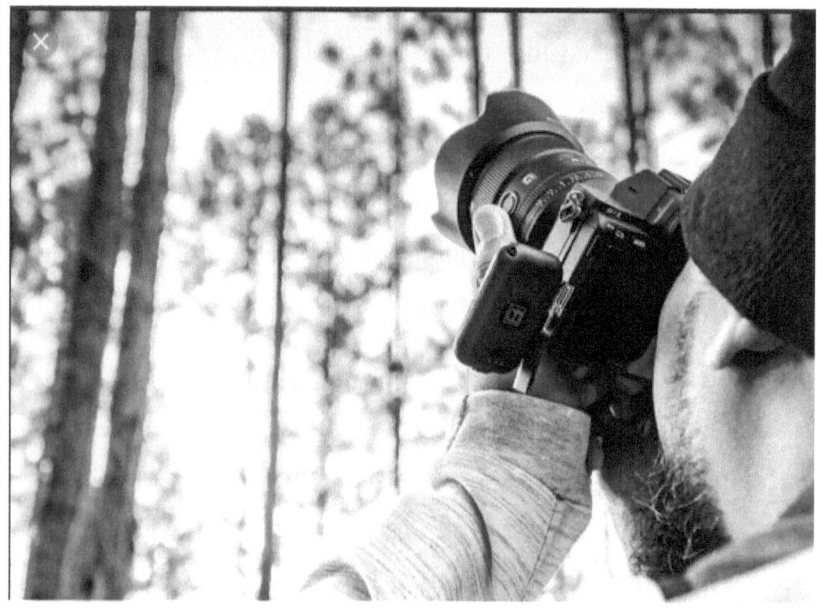

Smartphone photography can be used to tell the story of our lives through images and videos. It can be used to record how we see the world around us, which is what allows us to capture and share beautiful, high-quality photos taken with the camera we carry along with us. It's essential to gain the skills and know-how to generate high quality, creative images that take your phone photography to a whole new level.

Professional high-quality images are critical to marketing and branding strategies for small businesses. People are more likely to remember just 10 per cent of the information they hear, but some days later, if a good picture is combined with that information, they are more likely to retain about 65 per cent of that information.

High-quality photography is a pillar of brand strategy from website graphics for social media to content marketing, but an expensive photographer does not necessarily have to be hired to produce professional shots. With the technology built in the iPhone cameras and editing apps, professional-looking photos can be achieved using just your iPhone Pro or Pro Max.

Basic Photography and Camera Features

Smartphone photography makes it possible to achieve great results with just a little tweak here and there in your settings. We will examine some of these instructions and learn how Apple has improved on them to create amazing results for its phone users.

First off, although many new users tend to depend on your phone's default auto mode when taking photos, you can, however, achieve sharper images if you can control specific settings like focusing on a subject whose picture you want to take by taping to indicate where you want your focus to be. By modifying or changing various other things in an image, the overall quality of your pictures can be improved. Although different phones have different ways of setting them, most should be able to let you control the focus, exposure, white balance, and ISO. With the help of this book, you will now be able to control most of those settings on the iPhone 11 Pro and Pro Max easily.

It is also essential to note that some cameras, both lock the exposure and focus together, leaving you dependent on wherever you want to target. As for white balance, there are four settings to choose from, and it is best to match them according to the environment you are shooting to light up your photos better or to allow for more creative pictures, playing around is allowed. For example, Cloudy and Daylight are more suitable for outdoor shoots, whereas Fluorescent and Incandescent are used for indoor shots or photos. That said, you can choose to mix them up to create different tones and moods for more creative images.

If you set your resolution to high, you can get a higher resolution of your picture and, therefore, better quality. Try to move as close as possible to the subject when taking photographs with a smartphone camera, instead of zooming in when taking a shot, this helps to get sharper images. You will get better-resolution by having photos cropped than by zooming-in.

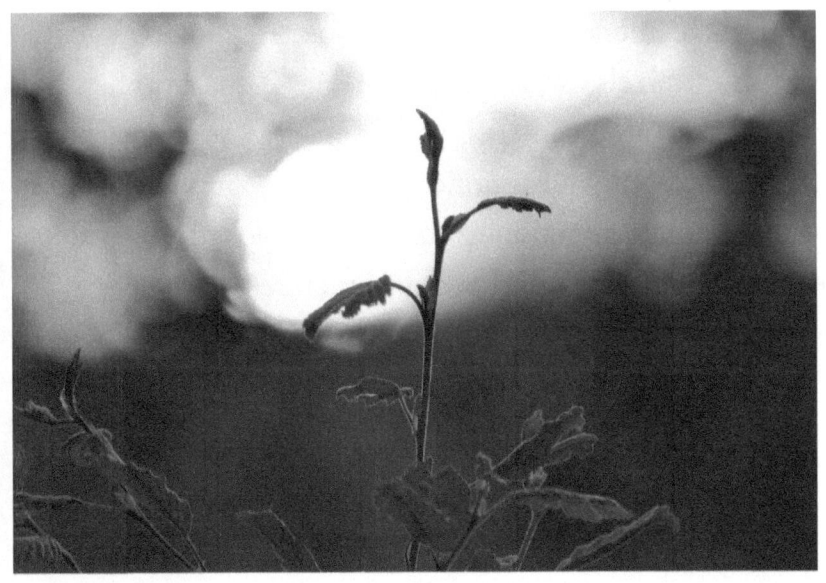

iPhone 11 Pro and Pro Max are an improvement in producing high-quality images with the iPhone because of its wide-angle lens, which allows it to capture a wider range from a closeup shot. Of course, with higher resolution photos, you may now have the challenge of having enough storage to store them all on your iPhone 11 storage space.

Sure, the front camera makes it easier to take your selfies, however, that doesn't eliminate the fact that front cameras generally tend to have lower resolution specs than the back cameras, however, the iPhone 11 Pro and

Pro Max has overcome that challenge and has reduced the fear associated with the usual blur in front camera images.

The back camera, though, is still better equipped with more megapixels, with its powerful 12 megapixels for each of the three cameras, which ensures you can show off photos from your iPhone with better confidence. The front camera's function is majorly deployed for video conferencing, selfies, and personal pictures.

The iPhone 11 Pro and Pro Max take solid selfies, the camera app will crop in for a 7MP selfie for single selfies when held vertically and when held horizontally, it expands to a broader field of view with 12MP resolution for the group selfies. All four cameras on the iPhone 11 can record at 4k resolution at up to 60fps.

Developing Professional Photographs

Lenses are integral to the photo-taking and sometimes can have some dust on them, which you can do well to wipe out, and have them cleaned to remove any grime or fingerprint stains. You might be amazed as to what a simple cleaning action can do to your images, as it helps to get a clear picture. You can also opt to try detachable lenses to get the most from your phone camera because of the additional unique effects such as macro shots or fisheye shots you can get from them.

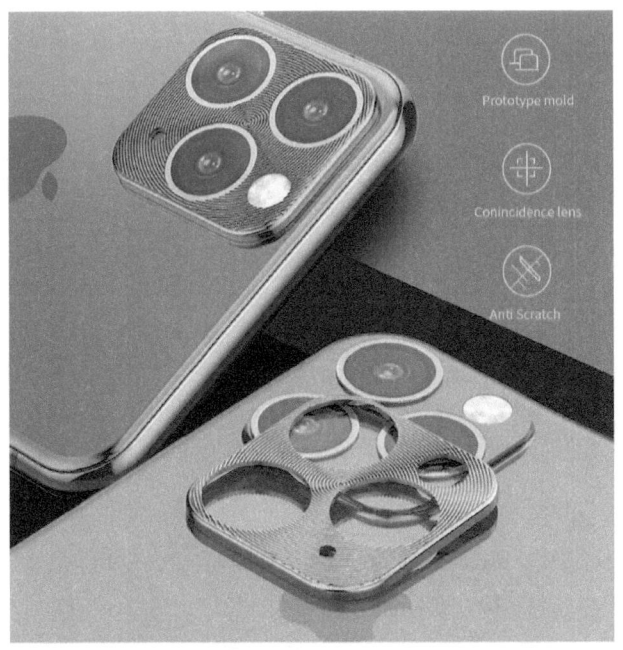

Your phone camera also comes with a relatively good stabilizing function, however, such a stabilizing role can only do so much, but when compared to the clarity afforded to you by tripods and monopods, you cannot but notice the difference. Tripods are ideal for slow shutter velocities, whereas the monopod is a single long staff allowing you to take a shot from far away. This is quite ideal for selfies. Most phone tripods are small and portable, like the GorillaPod and Slingshot, which also allows for mobility.

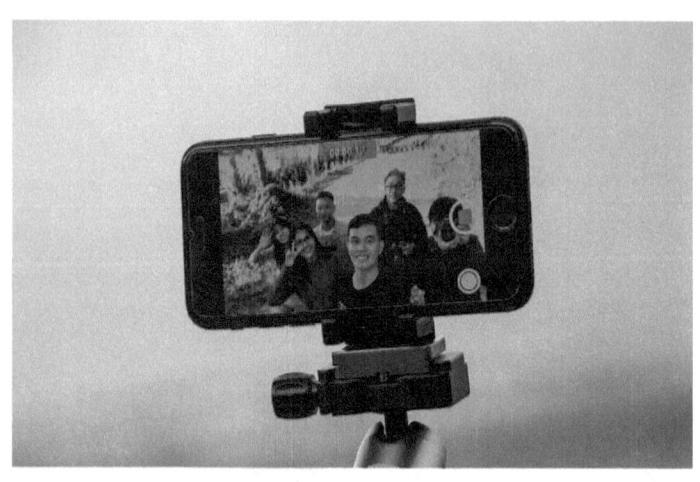

There are also tripods that you can wrap around poles and bars to let you take photos from a creative angle. The magic a detachable lens will do with your iPhone 11 camera knows no bounds. One of the most significant challenges with taking photos indoors is the lack of natural lighting. The proper amount of light will make food appear more appealing, bring more cheery facial expressions, create a more welcoming environment, and produce more appealing portraits. Where possible, try to take your photos under natural lighting, even though the iPhone 11 Pro and Pro Max have features that make it possible not to worry about this. It is, however, generally good photographic practice to be creative with your photos by staying close to the windows or doors when taking photos indoors and to sources of light like neon signs or street lamps when snapping photos outdoors to have a clearer picture or an improvisation for your iPhone.

Enhancing your Photoshoot Quality

Also, it is always crucial to remember where your lighting source comes from as the general lighting rules are the same here as in DSLR photography. Just avoid backlight when taking pictures of people unless deciding to go for a silhouette effect. When you snap your subject using sidelight, it will capture texture and depth. Although many amateur photographers rely on the flash from their cameras or phones to provide lighting, where possible, it is always best to avoid using your flash for lighting as your camera flash is almost too harsh and rarely helpful. Instead, you can adjust by increasing your camera's exposure and ISO levels. This is usually what sets professional photographers from amateurs. Alternatively, you can decide to use an external flash like iBlazer or Lightstrap.

Nothing beats composition when you want to have an attractive picture. Learning how to do some basic composition like Rule of Third, leading lines, scale, framing to name just a few can significantly improve the quality of your photoshoot, and this is also discussed in the latter part of this guide. Understanding the rules of composition, breaking them, playing with other aspects like lighting and angles, will surely get you to begin to create truly amazing and creative images.

Speaking of angles, shooting from a different perspective can sometimes make your subject more flattering, exciting, and fabulous. It can also present a different point of view and sometimes highlight details not captured. Most phones have panoramic mode, and you would expect that the iPhone 11 Pro and Pro Max would also have it. You can take or snap your 180-degree images, such as Photosynth (iOS) and Autostitch Panorama (Android), with an app. They are great for taking landscape photos, provided your hand is steady enough to grab a well-taken picture.

Also, moving objects don't make for a good panorama, as this can lead to a blurry image or lack of focus image. Speaking of snapping photos of moving objects and people, they are not going to keep still while your phone camera snaps. To retain and keep records of this perfect moment, activate your phone or camera app's burst mode. It will take multiple pictures at a time, which will increase the possibility of snapping at least one clear image you desire. Suffice to say, this is an excellent mode for catching kids and pets in motion.

Great Photoshoots Tools

As mentioned before, your iPhone camera has a plethora of functions. You may consider getting some third-party camera apps to boost the quality or attractiveness of your pictures. Apps like Camera+ (iOS) and Capture Free (Android) have additional features alongside standard phone settings, and others are also discussed in the later section of this book. Some of them have functions or features that are more specialized, like Slow Shutter Cam (iOS), Night Cam, and HDR (iOS, Android). Many of these third-party apps are regularly updated with new features, filters, modes, and options as well, and you can decide to update these apps regularly, this beats getting a new phone to get more photo-snapping features to play with. Often, when taking a photo, there's only so much we can monitor, and a lot of the improvement has to come from using photo-editing software after the pictures are taken.

Some apps like Camera+ and Camera FV-5 (Android) come coupled with a photo editor and offer amazing features. Photoshop Express (iOS, Android) and Pixlr Express (iOS, Android) perform editing functions like crop, straighten, rotate, flip and removing red-eye, even some of these functions have been incorporated into the new iPhone 11 Pro and Pro Max Camera app. If your major interest is in filters, you can try Snapseed (iOS, Android) and VSCO Cam (iOS, Android).

This is quite instructive to take quality pictures with your iPhone, and you can also heighten your enthusiasm a bit by playing around with certain interactive filters like Spotliter that allows you to add filters not only to pictures but also to videos, as you capture and record the memorable moments in your life.

Justification for iPhone 11 Pro and Pro Max Photography

The iPhone is a fantastic device for snapping pictures. It has excellent hardware, smart software, and it's easy enough to use. It allows for improvisation in every way possible to achieve a superb fill of creative images.

In other to achieve excellent outputs, there are some precautions to put in place. To document a beautiful memory with your iPhone 11 Pro and Pro Max, then it's essential to learn to use your iPhone camera shortcut.

Swipe up on the iPhone camera shortcut from the locked screen, and you can immediately start taking pictures with no delay. You can do a similar thing even with an app on as well by sliding up the Home screen from the bottom to start Control Centre. Then tap the Camera button to quickly respond to any movement you intend to capture with your amazing iPhone 11 Pro and Pro Max Camera.

Note that the default Apple Camera app offers a range of photography styles, including panoramic and square mode photography. It may sound like common place, but it helps if you shoot in the publishing mode you plan to use, for example, if your plan is to post pictures on Instagram, it is fitting to snap in square mode instead of shooting in photo mode and then having to trim the image later. It is always better to compose your picture better, instead of attempting to concoct unused surrounding after the fact.

Your iPhone has a grid option available, which can aid you in lining up photographs so that they follow the rule of thirds, which can be essential to achieving quality images. You can turn this option on by checking out Settings > Photos & Camera and enabling the Grid switch.

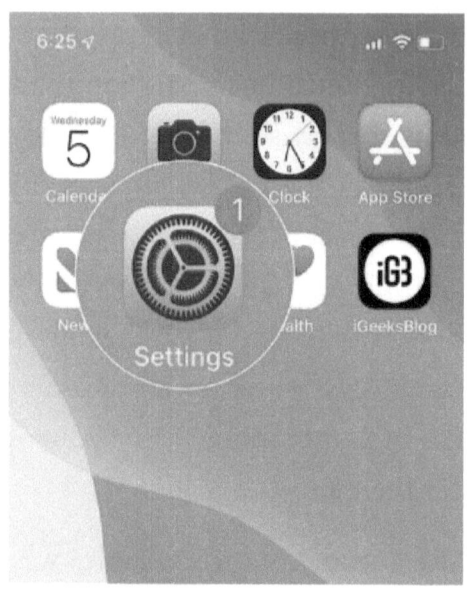

Grid options are always an excellent feature to have on, so that it serves as an aid and a reminder to apply the rule of thirds, but you can switch it off at any time by returning to the Photos & Camera Setting's screen of your iPhone.

The iPhone 11 Pro and Pro Max like some other versions of the iPhone have an incorporated feature named the High Dynamic Range, or HDR for short. This feature enables taking pictures that have an intense contrast light sources; this means a brightened sunset against a darkened mountain and still take excellent photography without any high exposure to light or underexposure as a result of darkness to the picture. Your iPhone performs this by snapping several images in quick succession at different exposures, then merging them to create a beautiful, unified image. You'll be able to turn HDR on or off manually from the Camera app.

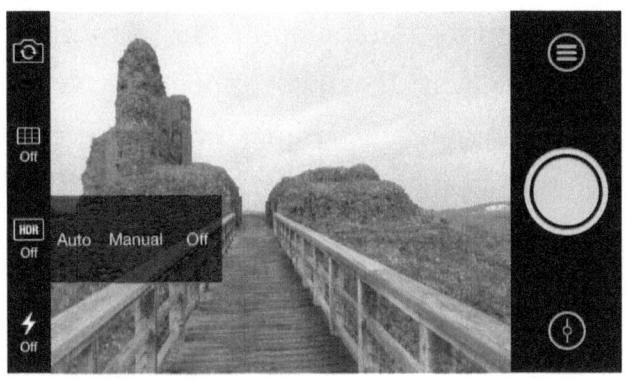

HDR uses data from your iPhone's sensors as you point your gadget at a subject to decide when a picture might require HDR adjustment, and at this point, the HDR mode can get turned on. (You will surely know if HDR is used by the little yellow 'HDR' box that appears at the bottom of the screen.)

Developing Professional Photoshoots

To create quality photos from your iPhone 11 Pro and Pro Max, it is essential to always keep the light in mind and see how it affects your photography. The Rule of thirds, balancing the elements of your photo, and placing your interest in the center of the photograph are also essential aspects of photography to abide by. You can use the leading lines to serve as a guide to your eyes to your subject or interest and balance your photographs to lines of symmetry by using reflections of water or surfaces.

Another way to develop iPhone professional photographs is by taking Action Photography like capturing fast-moving subjects using the burst mode in your phone. You do this by tapping the shutter button for capturing still photos and swiping it to the left, and your iPhone 11 Pro and Pro Max will enter burst mode, and you can take multiple shots in a row.

You can also get a better iPhone photography professionalism by investing in other accessories. These accessories may include fisheye, external lens, tripod, monopod, camera app, HDR app, and so on. It is always good to keep your photos simple and not to overcomplicate things to add a ton of subjects and detail as you try to focus on the subject.

Shoot from a Low Angle

Taking a great photo involves thinking outside the box, which can include shooting from a low angle. This way, you'll be able to shoot from a distinctive viewpoint removing undesirable diversions and making the subject stand out against the plain background, and also, you'll be able to show exciting points of interest from your photoshoot.

Capturing Close-up Details

This is also another great way to develop savvy photography photos with your iPhone to take close-up patterns, textures, and colors to bring life to your photos.

Chapter 2

Meet iPhone 11 Pro and Pro Max Camera

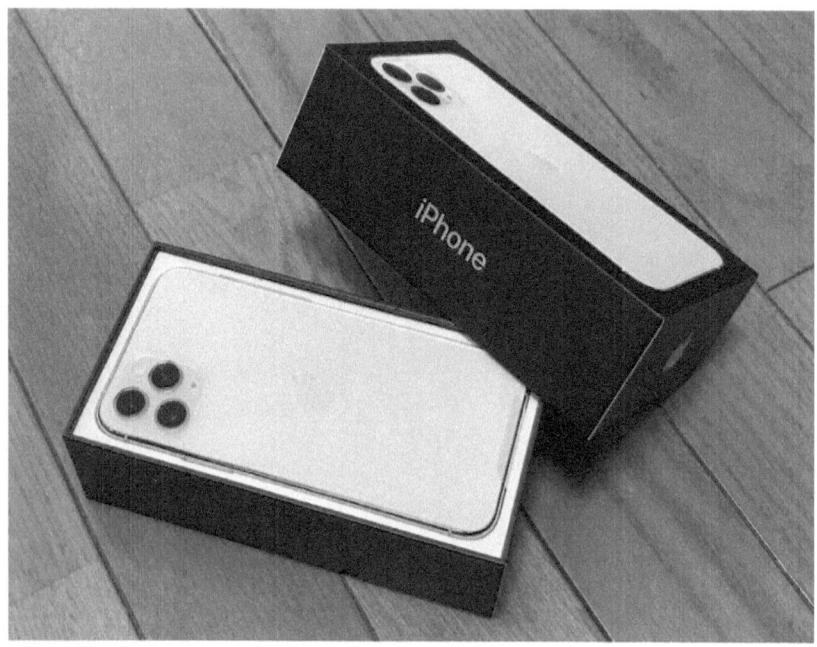

The iPhone 11 Pro and Pro Max have a new ultra-wide camera. The primary wide-angle camera still being 26mm focal length, 6-element wide-angle f/1.8 aperture with optical image stabilization, and 12MP sensor. It has better light sensitivity and also a hundred per cent Focus Pixels for face detection autofocus, which means that all fractions of the pixels in the camera sensor are high-resolution focus.

The front-facing TrueDepth Camera system of the iPhone 11 Pro and Pro Max is a new 12MP camera, which makes it possible for improved efficiency of its Face ID recognition, which is now up to 30 per cent faster and able to work from wider angles. It also supports 120 fps slo-mo videos, allowing users to capture slo-mo selfies (slofies).

The telephoto camera has a 2mm focal length and 6-element wide-angle, larger f/2.0 aperture, which captures 40% more light. The new ultra-wide-angle camera comes with a 13mm, 5-element lens, f/2.4, and 1200 fields of view, which videos real depth data to the wide-angle portrait mode, allowing for better landscape shots and tight shots that can capture more without having to adjust the position of your iPhone.

The broader field of view allows you see to and take note of details outside your image frame. The iPhone 11 Pro and Pro Max have an added opportunity to capture real videos, with much more details and free switch in motion. It allows you to have the capacity to shoot 4K videos with an extended dynamic range and cinematic video stabilization at 60 fps, which is the best quality you can get from any smartphones.

If you are unable to capture everything in the picture, you can zoom out to take advantage of the new ultra-wide camera to capture more of the scene. This makes it look like you took a shot by taking some steps backwards to capture more of the scene even though you did not take that backward step. Make sure you have Photos Capture Outside the Frame Settings switched on to use this feature, this is what enables you to shoot with the telephoto to have that extra field of view with details that will be captured with the wide-angle and also captured from the ultra-wide-angle lens.

Your iPhone 11 Pro and Pro Max, by default, helps you fine-tune details of your subject and your background with the Smart HDR. The phone employs machine learning to identify faces in your shot and relight them smartly. It brings lightning and detail to the faces while maintaining color variation in the background.

If you suddenly see something you want to capture as a video while taking photos, with a feature like the QuickTake, you do not need to switch modes any longer, just long-press the shutter to enable recording. Scroll right to lock it so that it can continue recording and snap left to take burst photos.

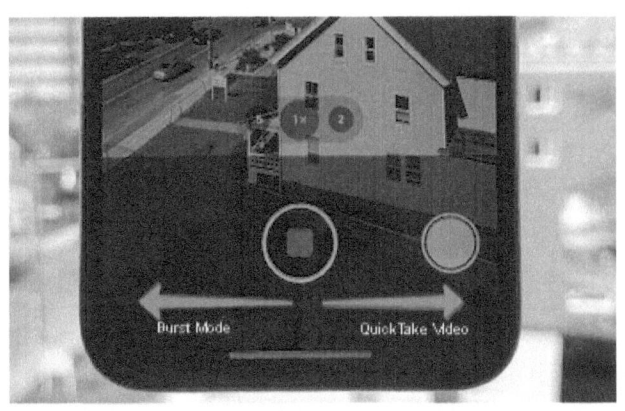

Knowing When to Use the Flash

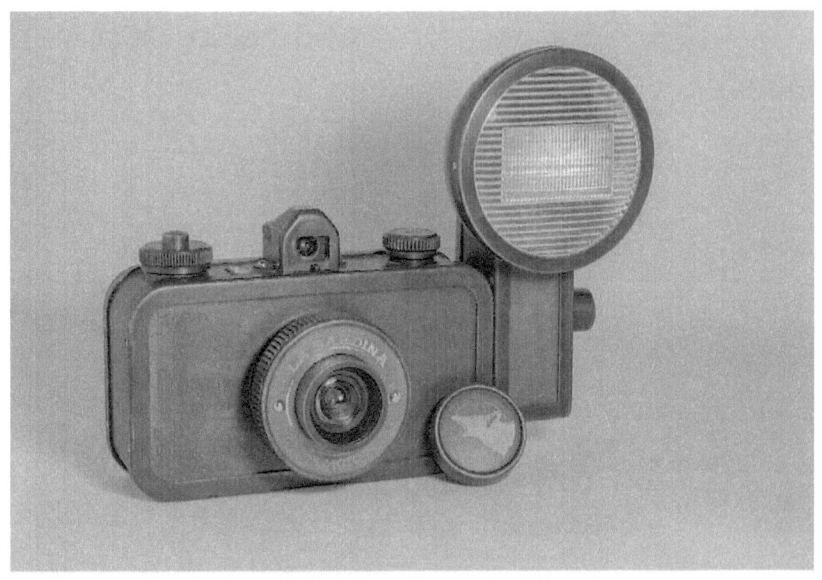

While taking a photo, you may opt to use flash to add more light to your photo, especially in dark scenes. However, knowing when to and when not to use flash is a vital photography skill to have. These are a few suggestions as to when to use the flash on your iPhone.

Daytime Outdoors

While taking photos during the daytime, the flash can act as a second light source, filling in areas where the image is underexposed due to the camera's metering mode prioritizing a different part of the frame.

Motion Freezing

The flash allows you to freeze the motion in a photo with a short burst of light, which works, especially while shooting in low light.

Ultra-wide Panoramas

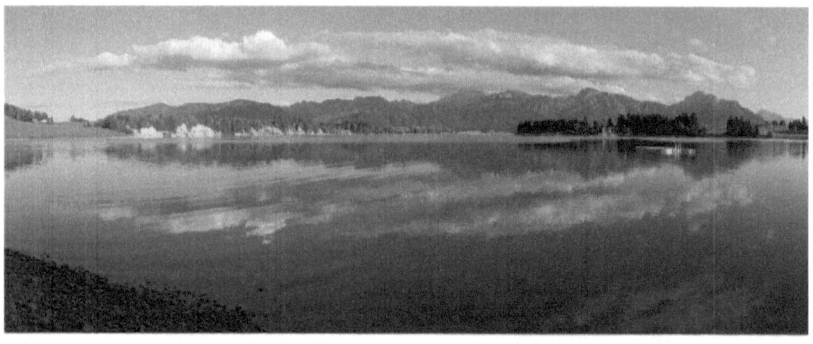

Great pictures of wide areas can be taken with the Panorama feature. Tap the Camera app to open it and slide the screen from top to bottom until the Pano option is chosen. You can then use the rectangular box that appears across the middle of the screen with an arrow that points in the direction you want the photo panned. The direction of the panorama can, however, be swapped by tapping the arrow.

Tap the take picture button and sweep across your scene, using the arrow to keep level. Once you're happy, tap the take picture button again, and it will be saved to the Photos app.

Rule of Thirds

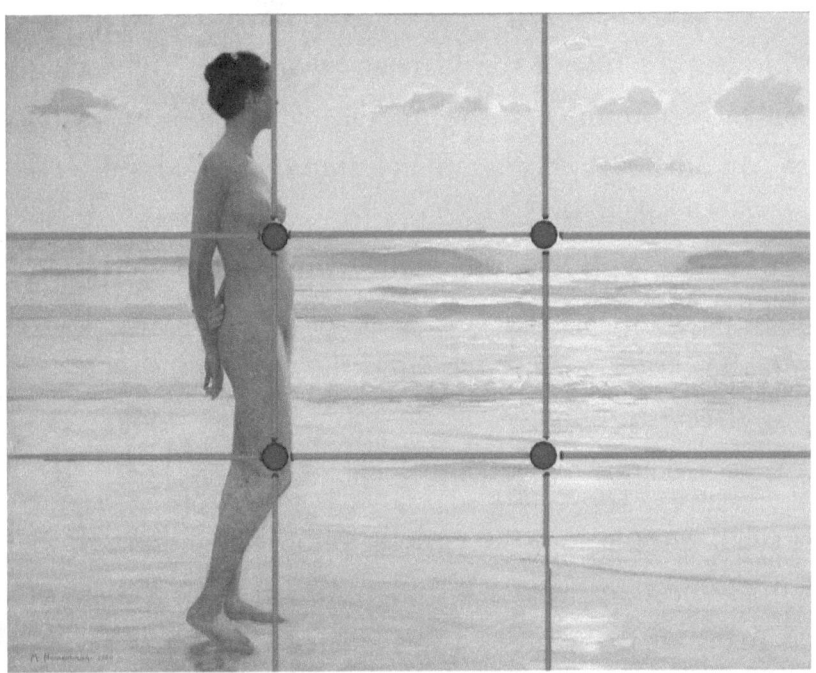

The rule of thirds can also be referred to as the "rule of thumb," or a means to guide a photographer so that he can better compose an image or images like designs, paintings, media, and photographs.

In photography, the rule of thirds is a type of image composition in which an image is shared into thirds, upward and downward while the subject of the image is placed at the intersecting points of those dividing lines, or along one of the edges; the rule of thirds is considered one of photography most important technique of composition and perhaps the most popular.

Deploying the rule of thirds means that instead of having your subject framed in the middle, which is how many new or amateur photographers frame their shots, you instead visualize that your photo is divided into nine equal parts. You do this with two vertical and two horizontal lines so that you can take the picture away from the center and by targeting the line on either side. The effect of this is that your images look very professional and have a better feel.

You can have a look at various photos that have won awards, one thing you will find common among them is that many of them obeyed this rule of third. It is a very powerful photography tool used by many eminent photographers all over the world.

Fortunately, on the iPhone, you can easily display these grid lines within the camera app to make using the rule easy to deploy.

To switch on the gridlines, go into Settings -> Camera -> Grid. The next step of using the "Rule of Thirds" is to open the Camera and the compose by thirds and then shoot your photo.

Leading Lines

A leading line is a line in your image that position your eye from one part of the scene to another. The most potent image arrangement is usually achieved when the lines lead your eye towards the focal part of your image. Leading lines are one of the most useful elements in smartphone photography, even DSLR photography. They can be used to create good pictures with a strong visual impact.

This photographic concept helps draw the eye into the picture while giving prompt focus to the viewer's attention on the main subject. It is also an excellent means of creating depth of field and symmetry in your image.

For example, a path leading towards a person within or outside distance, a bridge with a train at the end of it, a row of trees with a building at the end, or a subway tunnel with lights leading your eye to someone in the distance, a leading line inviting you to follow the line through the image. Even if the lines don't lead to a particular object, lines leading into the distance are still beneficial in any image composition. The lines depict the focal point of your iPhone image.

A picture can contain multiple lines, and this often results in exciting patterns being formed to create beautiful models, the strongest compositions will be the point of intersection, giving your image an elegant look. Lines are quite ideal because a well taken shot with a strong leading edge appeals to even the most disinterested viewer.

Leading lines can create a different visual experience that can exceed your expectations by instantly catching the viewer's attention. The leading edge immediately gives you a hint of what a particular image is about by drawing your eye to the most crucial part of the picture, and it's a great way of creating a sense of depth in your photographic scenes. This concept will help you compose your image. If there's a particular object in the image you want to emphasize, you can place it along the leading line or at the end of it, thereby giving it focus.

Leading lines will also assist you when you have to decide where to position yourself before taking your shot, to have a beautiful aligned image. If you are shooting a road, for example, the most natural position would be to stand in the center of the road along the central line and have your picture well-focused and ensure you capture essential details.

Recomposing Photos and Videos

Recomposing picture is when you take a picture, you carefully frame your shot and place your subject somewhere in the frame before you take the picture. In other words, you have been able to compose the shot. Recomposing simply means framing your shot first (for example, to acquire focus), then moving your iPhone camera to reposition your subject somewhere else in the frame.

For example, let's say you started by placing the subject in the center of the frame and focusing on the subject and tapping your screen to lock the focus, instead of having a boring shot with your subject in the dead center, you could have a much better composition by placing the subject a little to the side.

In other words, you are recomposing your shot. Usually, most people do not bother to recompose their shots when using their phones, but with the iPhone 11 Pro and Pro Max, this feature can come in handy. The iPhone 11 Pro and Pro Max cameras come with a bunch of focus points, which are scattered across the screen, as seen when composing a shot, the easiest thing to do is typically to move the focus point to the desired area where the subject is, acquire focus by tapping your screen and then take a picture.

In addition to this, the primary focus point is always the most accurate and precise in all phone cameras. This means that when light conditions are poor, your only chance to get acceptably sharp images might be to use the center focus point and the flash coming off on the subject.

iPhone 11 Pro Series Ace iPhone 11

The iPhone 11 Pro and Pro Max are the latest Apple phones in existence as the phone's amazing features are innumerable. And this is no small feat when you consider all the great features Apple packed into the phone. Packed with its 12 megapixels three rear cameras, it means you are getting arguably the best cameras in the phone along with other leading performances and an OLED display that outshines most Android phones.

The iPhone 11 Pro Max may pretty much feel the same as the other iPhones 11 in the series, but with its larger screen and longer-lasting battery, it sure can differentiate itself. That larger screen offers extra width for broader and clearer pictures even though some people find it too big.

It features a huge 6.5-inch screen, super Retina XDR display with 2688-by-1242-pixel resolution at 458 PPI, triple-lens camera system that makes up its Wide Angle, Telephoto, and Ultra-Wide-Angle cameras respectively.

The iPhone 11 Pro Max, with its 6.5 inches screen size, is larger than the iPhone 11 pro screen's size of 5.8 inches, and it comes with a brighter OLED screen, comes with higher contrast, and a deeper black compared to the iPhone 11's LCD screen. Of course, the slightly smaller size of the iPhone 11 screen does make it a little easier to use, even though many customers prefer the larger iPhone 11 Pro and Pro Max.

The most significant difference you will notice is with the camera set up. The iPhone 11 Pro and Pro Max have three rear cameras that include wide-angle, telephoto, and ultra-wide-angle, while the iPhone 11 has just the wide-angle and the ultra-wide-angle cameras at the back. This means the iPhone 11 Pro and Pro Max can give you a wide range of pictures compared to the iPhone 11, especially if you are a picture enthusiast.

The iPhone 11 mainly captures details the same way the iPhone 11 Pro and Pro Max would, with just a few remarkable differences, though. There is a considerable similarity in the features of the iPhone 11 pro and pro max, the differences are minimal, especially when you look at the components that power both of them. There are a few other interesting variations that are difficult to catch merely by glancing at the phones.

The iPhone 11 Pro and Pro Max are both IP68 water-resistant; however, the iPhone 11 Max is rated for a depth of 4 meters (13.12 feet), whereas the iPhone 11 is only rated to a depth of 2 meters (6.56 feet) which is made possible by the advancement in Apple's technology. This may not matter much to some people, but this erases the worries around getting your new iPhone wet, it's also good to know that the iPhone 11 Max goes twice as deep.

The charging adapters are quite different too. Both the iPhone 11 Pro and Pro Max are capable of fast charging and can get up to about 50% charges in 30 minutes but only with a charger that is 18W or higher. Also note that the iPhone 11 Pro and Pro Max are packaged with an 18-watt charger, so it is advisable to take cognizance of this intending Speedlight charging capability; however, the iPhone 11 is packed with the same standard 5W charger.

In the end, Apple has a wide range of features to satisfy the desires of their users especially, with the introduction of the iPhone 11 Pro and Pro Max which makes it suitable for those who love the idea of having a phone with a large screen with an OLED display, that offers brightness and has good picture contrast.

Photography fans who want all the options available to them when shooting for documenting important events will most likely find the iPhone 11 Pro and Pro Max to be an excellent companion to have since it offers a wide range of options to boost your photographs.

And of course, for those who love class, want to stand out, and desire to have the newest and best iPhone that Apple has to offer, the iPhone 11 Max is your best bet.

The iPhone 11 is an excellent phone for most people considering its amazing features. The iPhone 11 screen is a little easier to use with one hand, and it is still an upgrade over the preceding iPhone, making it an excellent choice for anyone looking for a little more power and speed in their daily activities.

The Power of iPhone 11 Pro Camera

Your iPhone 11 Pro and Pro Max have three cameras at the rear, one more than the iPhone 11 and better than some other contemporary phones. The extra camera delivers an ultra-wide field of view equivalent to a 13mm lens on a full-frame camera, at 12-megapixels with an aperture of f/2.4, which is equivalent to some DSLR prime lens features.

Asides this, there are two other cameras, one of which has a primary 12-megapixel f/1.8 camera with optical image stabilization (OIS) and a wide range equivalent of a 26mm lens on a camera with a full-frame sensor and a third 2x telephoto camera that possesses a wide resolution of 12-megapixels, an aperture of f/2, OIS and a wide range view equivalent to a 52mm lens on a camera with a full-frame sensor, all to give you a quality output better than some high-value DSLR.

Another way to demonstrate the superiority of your iPhone 11 Pro and Pro Max camera in making your image excellent quality is that the phone builds on Apple's portrait mode. The iPhone 11 Pro and Pro Max can capture footages at 4K resolution at a maximum frame rate of 60fps, no other smartphone's video quality comes close when it comes to this level of quality.

Printing your photos from the iPhone 11 Pro and Pro Max

With its quality video on-the-go feature, your iPhone is indeed an equivalent of a DSLR and enough justification to see it as a powerful camera. You are also able to print your photos, you might have just taken a picture with your iPhone, and you wish to print it in hard copies just like a DSLR and expect to get a quality print.

To do this, open Photos, find the photo you want to print out for friends, then tap on the share button, go down and select print. Choose a printer, followed by the name of the printer that you want to add to the iPhone. The printer will now be added to the device and then you will see the print screen if you have a compatible computer that allows you to print. Tap the plus or minus buttons to adjust how many copies you want to print, and then, Tap on Print and off you go with your hard copy picture. This is indeed what a digital camera can do, and your iPhone offers this.

Chapter 3

Relevant Camera Settings to Know in Your iPhone

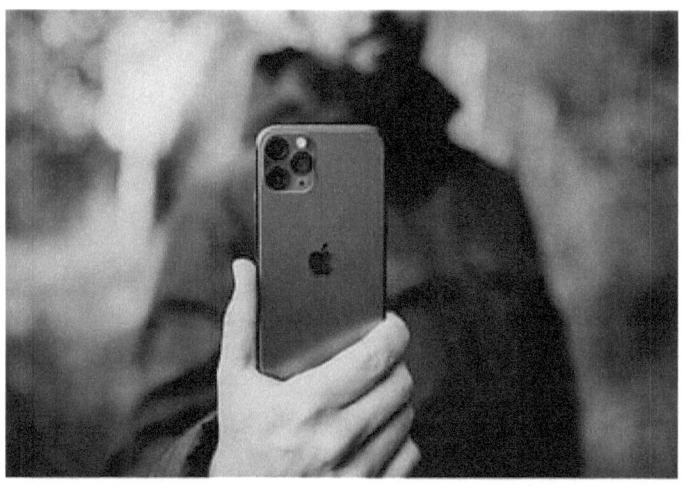

With the iPhone 11 Pro and iPhone 11 Pro Max, Apple has managed to deliver an iPhone that outperforms other flagship Android smartphones in the camera department. The new iPhones come packed with significant camera enhancements and features enough to make it the market leader.

While most iPhone 11 Pro and 11 Pro Max users will already know about the new Night mode, there are other camera settings that are also important to be known about. You can also turn the flash on or off by tapping the lightning button, then tap the chevron and tap the lightning button below the frame to choose Auto, On, or Flash Off.

Frames per Second and Resolution

When Apple announced the iPhone 11 Pro and 11 Pro Max, it made a huge deal about the fact that one could record 4k videos @ 60fps (an image with a resolution of 3840x2160 pixel that is displayed 60 times per second) from any of the three camera lenses of the iPhone. Most smartphones that offer a triple multipurpose camera system only allow users to record videos at the rate of 4k at 30fps.

You can adjust the video recording resolution on your iPhone 11 or 11pro max by clicking Settings - Camera - Record Video, this is easy and faster. From here, select the 4k at 30fps or 4k at 60fps option. When you use your iPhone 11 Pro or Pro Max in taking a photo with its primary camera, it will simultaneously capture a photo with the ultra-wide-angle camera when it deems it necessary. The ultra-wide-angle picture, even though it stays hidden, will remain saved for at least another 30 days, and it can become useful if you need to readjust your picture frame.

Using the crop tool, you should use the straighten and perspective tools of the built-in photo editor app, with these tools, you will gain access to the ultra-wide-angle photo which allows picture framing with regards to preferences.

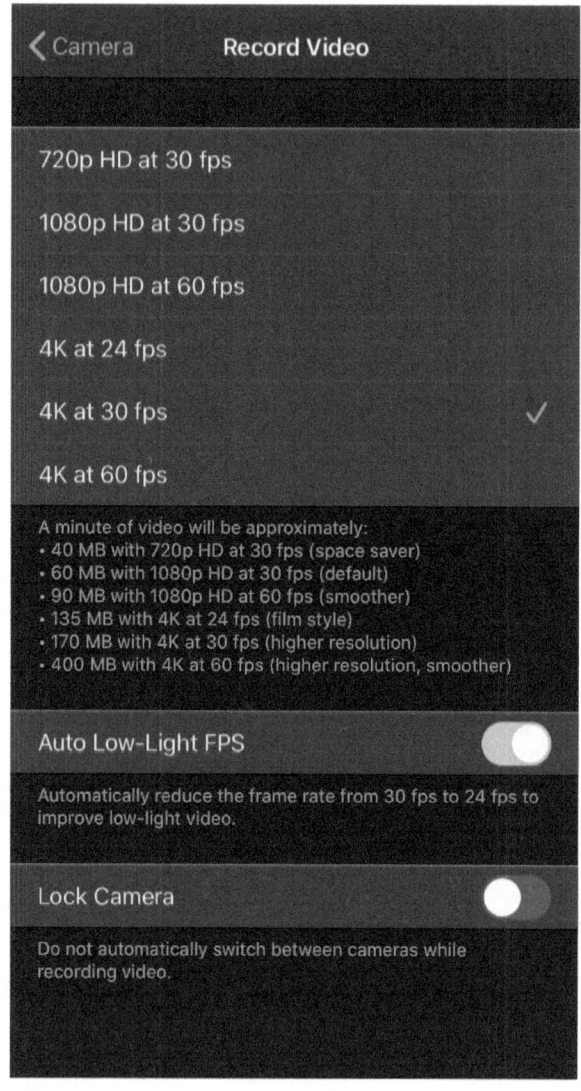

In most cases, your iPhone, by default, helps adjust your photo by using the image details captured from the ultra-wide-angle camera to enhance it. As such, the picture will have a blue Auto badge on its top-right corner showing it has been edited.

Accessing More Toggles

If your iPhone is mounted vertically, click the arrow at the top of the screen to reveal all the toggles. The arrow will change direction and show different toggles, such as flash, live images, aspect ratio, timer, and filters. You can tap the button again to hide them once you are done adjusting. Alternatively, you can also swipe across the viewfinder to reveal the toggles hidden.

Post Ultra-Wide-Angle Camera Editing

The iPhone 11 Pro and Pro Max models have an ultra-wide-angle camera that can be used to take some astonishing dramatic photos. There is a hidden feature that the ultra-wide camera enables. These functions can be used to zoom in on a frame that you are taking with the large or telephoto lenses after you have taken the picture. In other words, if you were taking a group photo, but snapped the photograph without everyone in the frame and failed to realize this until later. You can open the Photo app and use the crop tool to zoom out, bringing some of the subjects that were missed back into the picture. To use this feature, you will need to open the phone Settings app and select Camera. Then you scroll down to where you can turn on Photos Capture Outside the frame.

This feature allows you to capture any information captured outside the frame which you can use later, the phone automatically deletes these images after 30 days. In any case, if you attempt to zoom out on a photo, and nothing happens, you'll be able to select Edit, then tap on the three-dot symbol in the top right corner and select utilize content outside the frame. If your image has been cropped and straightened, a warning about resetting your previous crops will pop up, then tap to accept it, and you can edit the ultrawide shot.

Depending on how you take the photo, your iPhone will either have an ultra-wide shot around the main photo (which is when you can zoom out on it), or it will capture two distinct photos and only show the ultra-wide version when you specifically request for it using the menu display option.

As emphasized earlier, the iPhone 11 has an ultra-wide-angle camera and a wide camera. The iPhone 11 Pro and iPhone 11 Pro Max have the same cameras, along with a telephoto camera that covers for a long-range shot. All three cameras are 12 megapixels, each with high cognizance for details around the subject.

Zooming with the iPhone Camera

Regardless of which of the two iPhones you have, the primary camera is the wide range camera, the option labeled '1x' in the camera app. If you need to switch between cameras, you'll be able to tap on the zoom alternative, which is either 0.5x or 2x. Your iPhone's viewfinder will instantly, by default, zoom in or out. Scroll up or down to zoom in and out using the iPhone 11's new camera setup, but you can fine-tune just how far you want to zoom, in either direction, by long-pressing on the zoom level and then dragging the zoom tool with regards to your choice. Using the zoom wheel, you can zoom in from 0.5x to 10x anywhere.

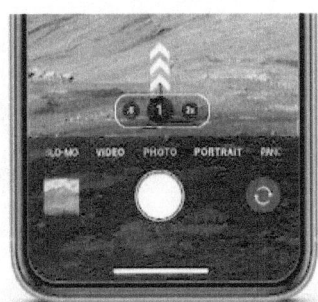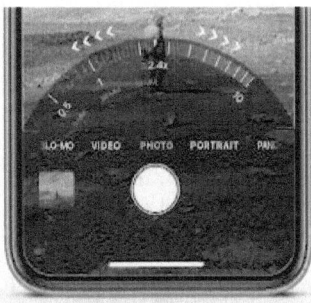

Note that if you pick anything else, but the three preset cameras zoom options that are 0.5x, 1x, 2x, you may experience lower photo quality due to the camera digital zoom, which has a lower quality than the fixed focal lengths of the built-in cameras.

Deep Fusion

Another critical feature to talk about is deep fusion. Deep Fusion is designed to work primarily in taking indoor pictures and in situations where the lighting is at a medium level where it is not too bright and not dark enough to activate Night Mode.

Deep Fusion works in the background and is automatic and cannot be turned on or off, but it is disabled when you have 'Photos Outside the Frame' turned on.

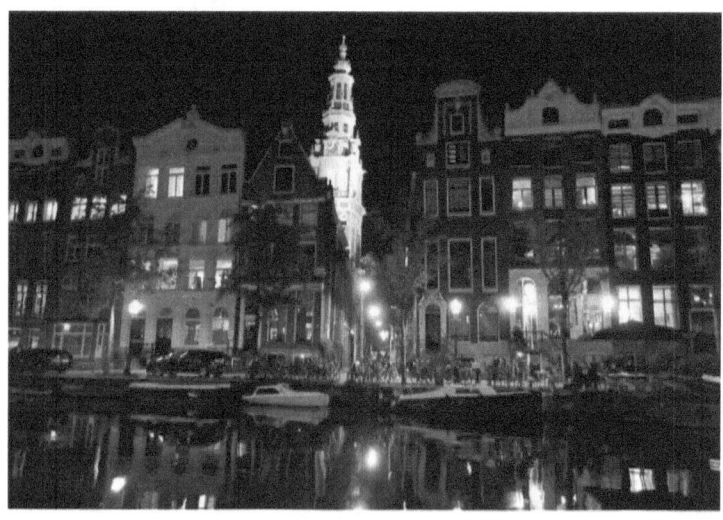

Deep Fusion on the iPhone 11 Pro and 11 Pro Max utilize the onboard A13 chip combined with machine learning for its pixel-by-pixel processing of photos, detail of images, optimizing images for texture, and reduction of noise on each part of an image.

Night Mode

The new Night mode is one of the major camera functions of the iPhone 11 Pro and iPhone 11 Pro Max. This function significantly contributes to improving the quality of pictures taken in low-light situations

Night mode automatically activates itself by being dependent on the lighting conditions. Numerous highlights of night mode can be customized too. Depending on the scene, the iPhone 11 Pro and 11 Pro Max will, when in night mode, choose the best exposure time by default. If you wish, this exposure time may be increased (or decreased) to tweak the final image quality.

To take advantage of Night Mode shots, Apple requires you to hold the camera steady for a few seconds while it takes multiple images of a scene to get the best possible lighting just like a DSLR so that the number on the icon is the number of seconds that the shot will last. You can choose a more prolonged exposure, which can slightly change the look of your image to a much brighter or darker depending on the other settings included.

Chapter 4

Maximizing the iPhone 11 Pro Camera

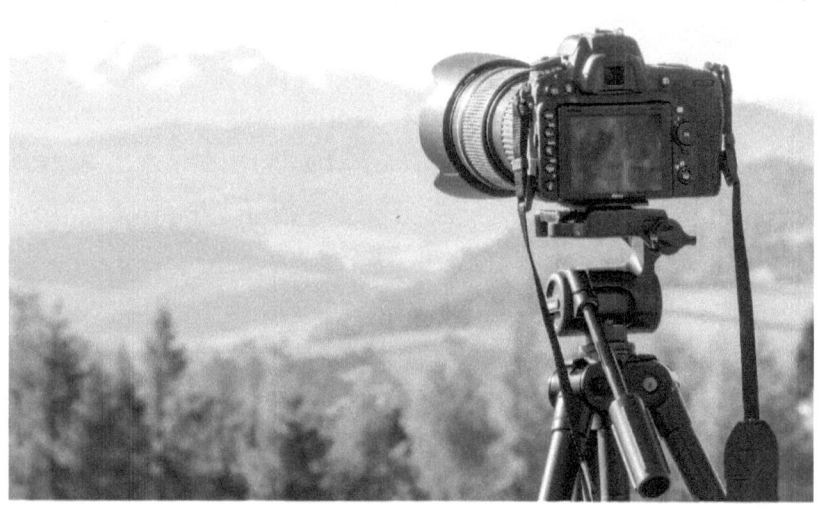

The iPhone 11 Pro and Pro Max cameras come with many features that can be used to perform various functions. The iPhone 11 Pro and Pro Max camera phones have revolutionized the notion of conventional photography, mainly because a camera phone that fits in your pocket is more comfortable to carry than carrying a DSLR camera. This phenomenon has brought about an influx of photo-sharing and photo-editing apps and has probably had a significant introduction of smartphone photographers and photography tools. There is a tendency to underestimate the capabilities of smartphone cameras, mostly because a lot of people have little understanding or idea about our smartphone cameras other than the megapixels it can take. In reality, knowing how to adjust specific settings, angles, and lighting, plus using other multi-functional apps and resources, it becomes possible to snap more interesting and exciting images that capture the essence of the moment than you'll ever get to a phone. The iPhone 11 Pro and Pro Max cameras deliver a wide array of features that help capture lovely moments, consequently, knowing how to optimize your iPhone 11 Pro and Pro Max to its full potential in making and documenting beautiful moments is an amazing skill to have.

Camera Functions on the iPhone 11

When you shoot in regular (traditional wide-angle) mode, Apple has updated its photo app to take advantage of the ultra-wide camera module.

As a result, right on your phone's display, you can see the scene you're shooting framed in a broader. This enables you to re-frame quickly without having to keep looking back and forth from your phone.

At 1x zoom, the iPhone deploys the ultra-wide lens to capture other areas of the photography scene, while at 2x zoom, the camera using the telephoto lens fills in the other additional space. The phone can also capture both images at once.

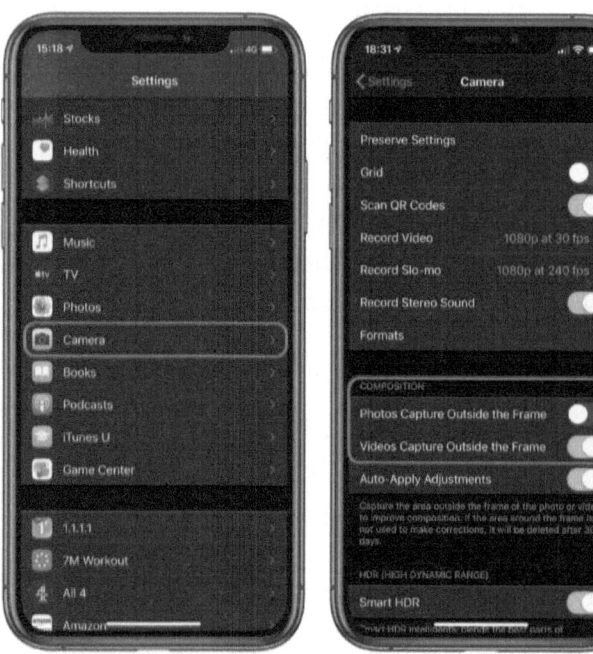

In addition to allowing you to choose between the different pictures taken later, it also provides for additional post-processing flexibility. For example, it is possible to re-frame an image to include areas that were not originally in the mainframe when captured. Partially cut off faces can also be fixed easily.

Photos Outside the Frame

Once you take a picture on your iPhone 11 Pro and Pro Max with the telephoto or wide-angle lens, there is a function that automatically captures what is outside the frame with one of the other lenses, and this is very useful in cases where you accidentally cut something out.

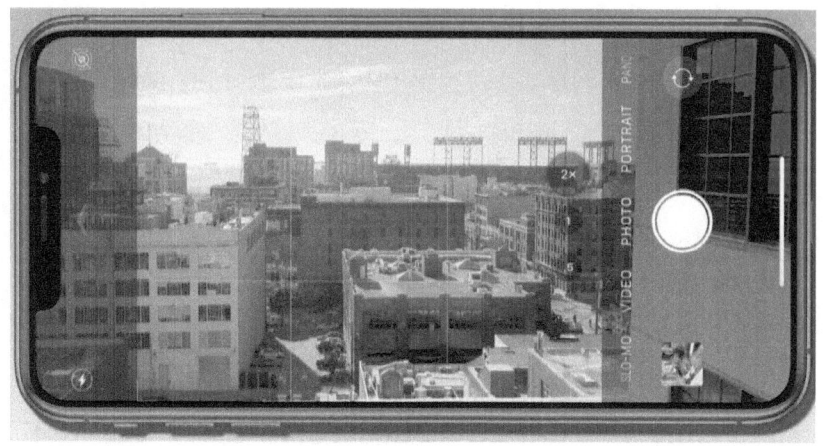

For this to work, the feature has to be turned on in the Settings of the Camera app's section to be able to take advantage of it when editing photos in the Photos app. It can come in handy for bunch shots, scene pictures, design, photographs, and other circumstances where you might need to alter the outlook of the image after taking a picture.

If you have got Photo Capture Outside the Frame turned on, you will be able to see more of the scene than the outline of the picture, this is what the Ultra-Wide camera sees and is the semitransparent border at the side of the picture taken by the wide angle lens, which allows you to be able to turn to the Ultra-Wide lens in case you like what's being shot outside the frame. Another great time to use the Ultra-Wide lens is if you've got a large gathering you would like to take a photo of and try to ensure everyone's included.

It's easier to squeeze everyone into the frame of the shot because of such a super-wide field of view, so nobody is cut out. If you frequently take pictures of buildings and designs, the Ultra-Wide lens helps in getting the whole structure into the outline. And with the 120-degree field of view, you can create some exciting takes on architecture. This is also useful for snapping pictures of building interiors, or any other beautiful scenery that can fit more into your picture frame.

Live Photos

On the iPhone 11 Pro and iPhone 11 Pro Max, Apple automatically groups Live Photos in succession together, letting you watch them video style. Live Photos bring movement in color photos to life. A Live Photo captures a 3-second image in motion instead of freezing a particular moment with a still image.

Live Photos can also be utilized to produce lovely and breathtaking, long exposure photos. To use the Live Photos, basically launch the built-in iPhone Camera app, and ensure it is on Photo mode at the base of the screen. At the top right of the screen is the Live Photos' icon (three circles).

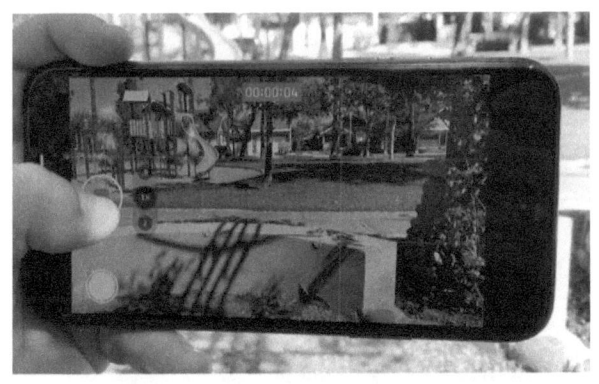

If it has no line through it, then the Live Photos is turned on. If a line is through the icon, tap it to toggle on the Live Photos. You can also pick all the live images you've taken, press the Sharing icon (a square with an arrow through it), and then choose to save as a video. Live Photos integrate high-resolution photos with video clips to make the pictures come alive.

Burst Mode

Burst mode is a term used to describe when your iPhone's camera takes a series of photographs in quick succession, at a speed of ten frames a second. It's a perfect way to shoot an action scene or an unusual occurrence, as you're often more likely to come up with the shot you've been looking for.

Hold down the shutter button for Quick Take mode and then swipe over to the left instead of the right towards the square displaying the last image you shot to activate

Burst Mode. In quick succession, Burst Mode will take several photos and then lets you pick the best of the bunch.

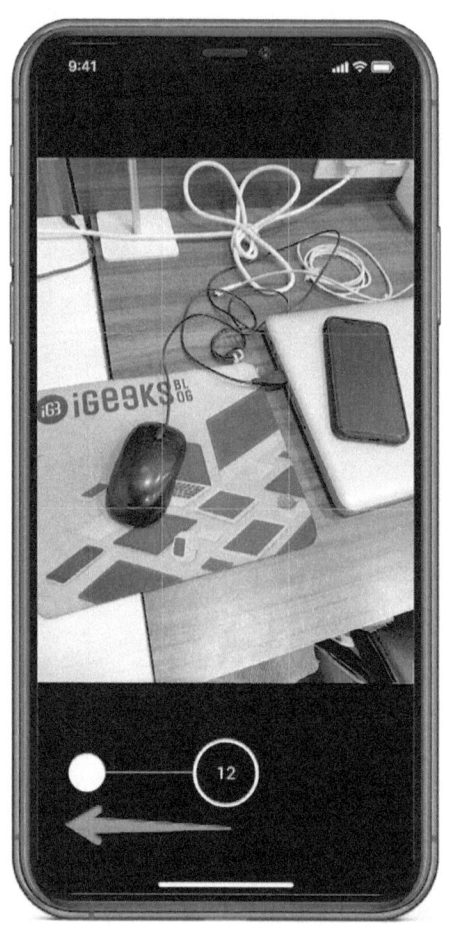

The timer increases within the initial position of the shutter, as long as you are holding it. Your burst photos automatically show in the Photos app in the Bursts folder. There you will also find the pictures in your main Photo Library.

Portrait Mode

The Portrait mode is the perfect tool for creating incredible iPhone portraits.

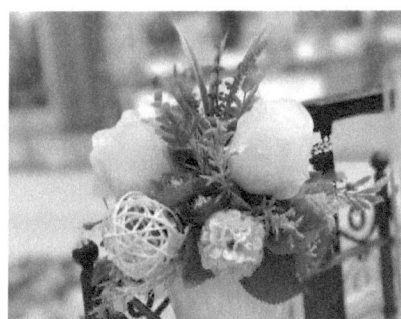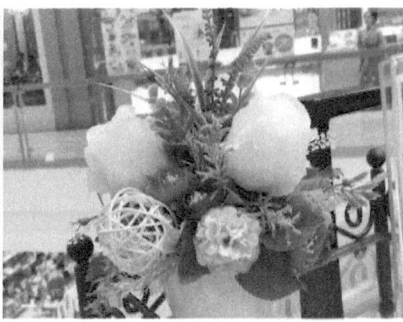

It employs intelligent computer programs to blur the background in your photographs. When utilizing Portrait Mode on the iPhone 11 Pro and Pro Max, you're not constrained to just one focal point as on the iPhone XS and XS Max.

Portrait Mode works with telephoto lenses as well as wide-angle lenses. You can use the portrait mode by swiping over to Portrait Mode to swap lenses and then tap the small "2x" or "1x" icons on the left side of the screen to zoom in or out. Using 1x mode will allow you to fit more into the picture, and it is ideal for scenes with multiple people or objects, while the 2x mode is great for zooming in on a single person, pet, or other similar things.

Portrait mode allows you to take professional-looking, jaw-dropping portrait photos by making the face of the subject to show up sharp, while the background looks blurred. Swipe at the bottom of the screen through the shooting modes and choose Portrait to use the Portrait Mode in your Camera app.

The regular 1x Wide lens is perfect for catching more of the scene in the background with that blurred look when you film in Portrait mode. It's ideal with a lovely backdrop when you want to catch your subject from the waist up.

You can have a headshots and close-up photo if you make use of the 2x telephoto lens for images you take with portrait mode. For pictures that involve Portrait mode, you have a few options, you can use the 1x or 2x button at the lower section of the viewfinder to switch between them while in Portrait mode.

Night Mode

Night mode is an essential feature of the iPhone 11 Pro and Pro Max that automatically takes advantage of the new wide-angle camera that comes with the iPhone 11 Pro models. It is equipped with a larger sensor capable of allowing more light into the sensor, thereby allowing for brighter pictures at low light. This will enable you to take photos at night, with lighting that was hitherto not possible on an iPhone, thanks to the latest technology and advanced machine learning algorithms.

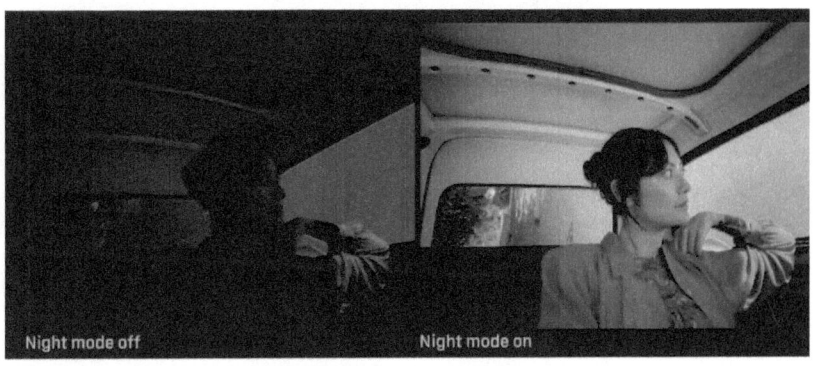

Night mode off · Night mode on

Although night mode brightens up images, it still retains the feeling of a night time, matching a picture's light and dark elements. The new Night mode utilizes the new sensor to create Night mode shots together with machine learning and the Neural Engine in the A13 Apple's Bionic processor.

When Night mode is activated, the cameras on the Apple flagship analyze the amount of light available, and then the iPhone selects the number of frames needed to create an appropriate image. For a predefined amount of time, the camera takes a series of pictures within such time frames, such as one second, three seconds, five seconds, or even longer in some cases.

Shooting Photos and Videos at the Same Time

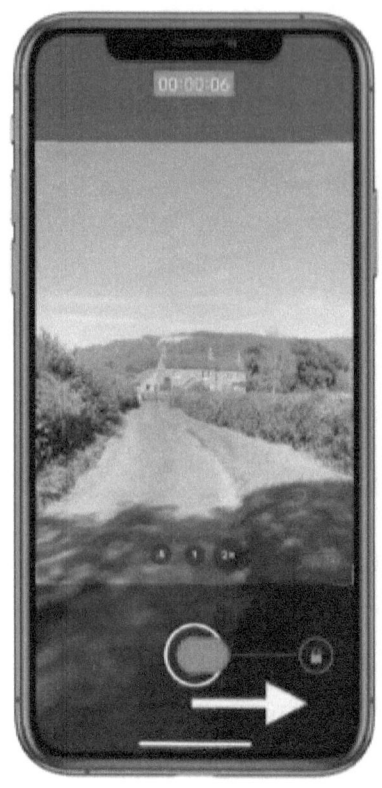

The iPhone 11 Pro and 11 Pro Max have a slick Quick Take highlight that allows for easy shooting of a video without having to swap over into video mode.

So, if you are taking photos and then decide instead to shoot a video, hold down the shutter button for it to begin recording. Sliding the shutter button to the right, and then releasing it, keeps video recording without having to hold the button. When the video recording is locked, the shutter button will appear at the center, which you can then tap to take a still photo when a video recording is ongoing. Whenever you're ready to stop recording, you can simply tap the record button again.

Zooming in and out on iPhone 11 Pro and Pro Max

On the iPhone 11 Pro and Pro Max, the Wide lens (1x) is the "normal" lens that you shoot with all the time on every iPhone since it came out.

The Ultra-Wide (0.5x), on the other hand, allows you to cover a wider view range than what the standard Wide lens can include. This fills the need for capturing landscapes. The Telephoto lens is only present on the iPhone 11 Pro and Pro Max, which is one of the reasons your latest iPhone stands tall in the hall of fame for iPhones and other smartphones.

With the Telephoto lens, you can go 2x optical zoom for a close shot at the subject. While you can zoom in further than 2x, it switches to digital zoom after the 2x, which means a reduction in photo quality. If there is a need to zoom in, try not to do more than a 2x zoom.

The image area outside the frame won't appear when it's too dark for the next-wider lens to function correctly because the ultra-wide-angle lens is designed to capture less light than the wide-angle, so without at least a moderate amounts of light, it isn't able to contribute.

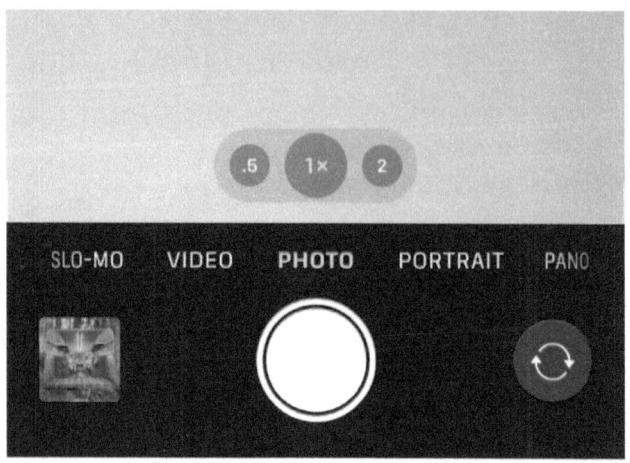

The over-capture also disappears when you're within several inches of an object. You can take a picture as you usually would with perhaps fewer worries about perfect framing, plus there's no extra step in the capture.

Adjusting Image Brightness

To change how bright you want a picture to be after you have taken the photo, you first open up the Photos app and then tap Edit. Then you can adjust the size of your photo, light, angle, add a filter, and do much more. You can go further and choose other adjustments by sliding the slider to change the strength and intensity of the brightness at the bottom of the screen. Swiping right will increase the brightness while swiping left will decrease it. If you don't like how your changes look, tap Cancel, and you can revert to the original, otherwise, tap Done to accept changes.

To adjust image brightness in the Camera app, open the Camera app. In the Photo mode (or Square), long-tap on the part of the image you want to focus on. With your finger still pressed on the screen, you can swipe up or down to alter the exposure. Swiping up makes it brighter with larger exposure, whereas swiping down allows for darker photos with lower exposure.

Deep Fusion Application

This is one Camera feature that works in the background and doesn't need to be turned on.

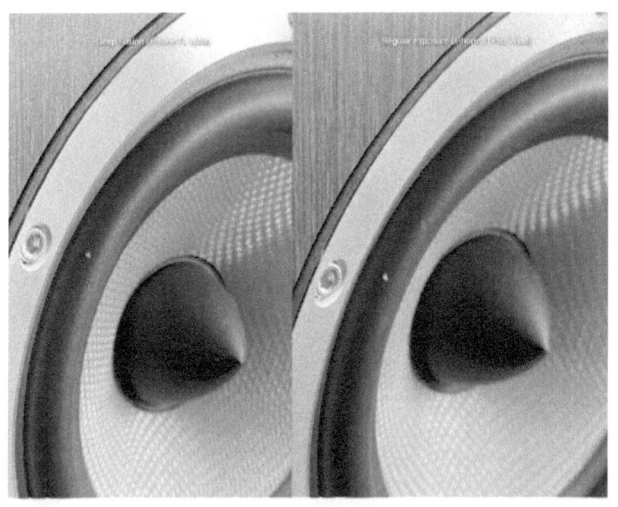

Deep Fusion uses machine learning and the A13 chip on the iPhone 11 Pro and 11 Pro Max for pixel-by-pixel processing of photos, optimizing for texture, details, and noise reduction in each part of an image.

This is going to be more noticeable in photos of people and pets where hair, fabric, and other aspects of textures are prominent.

Deep Fusion is designed to work primarily on indoor photos and in situations where the lighting is at a medium level, not too bright and not dark enough to activate the Night Mode on the phone. Deep Fusion is automatic and can't be turned on or off, but it does get disabled when you have Photos Outside the Frame turned on.

Chapter 5

Accessing More iPhone Camera Controls

On the iPhone 11 Pro and Pro Max, some controls of the camera are hidden by default. To display the icons, tap the up arrow at the top of the screen or swipe up on the viewfinder. Icons will appear near the bottom of the screen.

Some of the controls you will find in that settings include Flash, night mode (only available when there is low light), live photos, aspect ratio, timer, filters, and HDR. It is usually advisable to have the flash switched off unless you specifically want to make the scene lit up.

On the iPhone 11 Pro and Pro Max, you can capture photos using one of three aspect ratios: Square, 4:3 (standard rectangle), or 16:9 (wide).

The Timer icon also allows you to set the time it takes to press the shutter and capture the photo.

The Filter icon is used to change the color tone of your photo. To shoot without a filter, select the unchanged filter on the left. To hide these icons, tap the arrow downside the screen or scroll down the viewfinder.

Learning Video Settings

Whether you record videos on your iPhone once in a blue moon or are a notable vlogger, you will appreciate the option to adjust resolution and frame rate right from the Camera app in the new iOS 13.

To do that, you'd have to tap on **Settings -> Camera**, then you select either "Record Video" or "Record Slo-mo" and choose your preferred resolution from the options listed. You can also change the video resolution to create more space for other videos on your phone.

To adjust the Resolution directly from the Camera App on your iPhone 11 Pro and Pro Max, launch the Camera app. Now, select the "Video" option. Next, check out the Resolution controls for video at the top right of the screen.

To change the Video Capture mode to 60 fps instead of the standard 30 fps, open Settings. Navigate to the Camera options, then locate the setting to Record Video at 60 fps and then enable this by switching to the right.

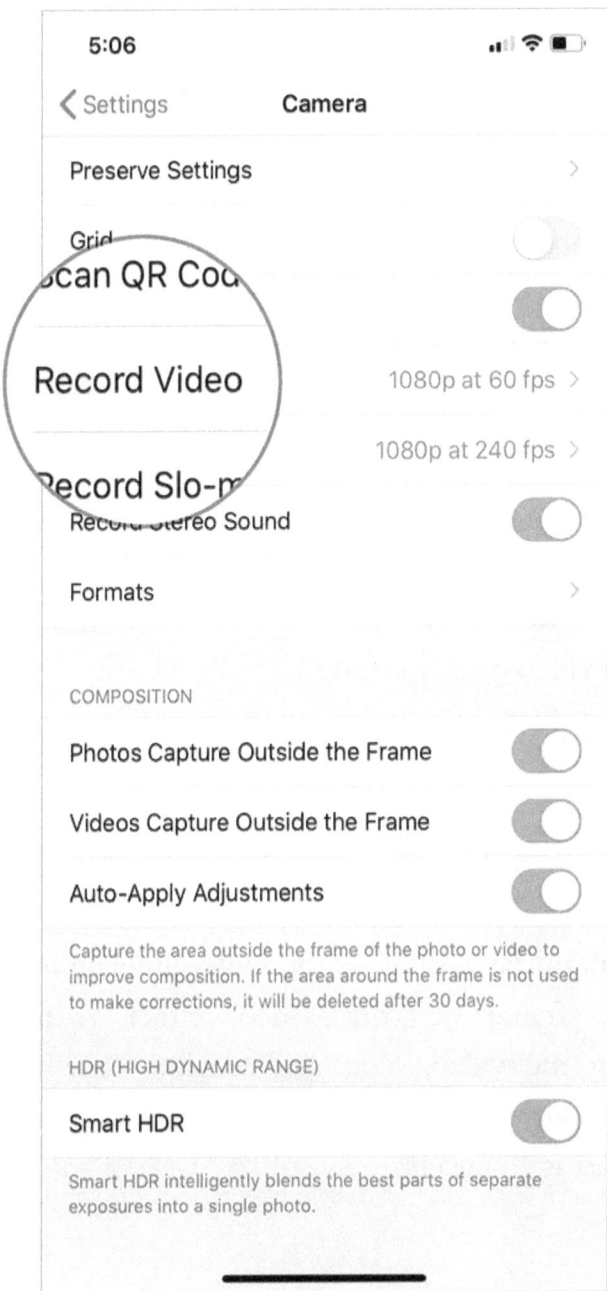

5:06

‹ Settings   **Camera**

Preserve Settings   ›

Grid

Scan QR Code

Record Video   1080p at 60 fps ›

1080p at 240 fps ›

Record Slo-mo

Record Stereo Sound

Formats   ›

COMPOSITION

Photos Capture Outside the Frame

Videos Capture Outside the Frame

Auto-Apply Adjustments

Capture the area outside the frame of the photo or video to
improve composition. If the area around the frame is not used
to make corrections, it will be deleted after 30 days.

HDR (HIGH DYNAMIC RANGE)

Smart HDR

Smart HDR intelligently blends the best parts of separate
exposures into a single photo.

Recording a Video

Choose Video mode in your Camera App. Tap the Record button or press either volume button to start recording. You can click the White Shutter button to snap a still picture when recording. Pinch to zoom in and out of the screen, then scroll the slider to the left. By pressing 1x or tapping .5x, you will be able to zoom out. To stop recording, press the Record button or push either volume button.

Video recordings switch to 30 fps (frames per second) by default. You can, however, change all that in Settings – > Camera > Record Video, you can pick various frame rates and video quality settings.

The faster the frame rate, and the higher the resolution, the better the resulting video file.

To edit your videos, open the Photos app and tap the video you want to edit. Just tap the edit icon and move the sliders on both sides of the video timeline to change the time frame of your video, either reducing or stretching the video. You can preview your video to monitor your progress. Then click on 'done' and save your video as a new clip.

Shooting a Time-lapse video

In some of the movies, TV show, or even a YouTube videos you may have watched, there's a good chance that you might have stumbled across a particular scene in the video that shows people walking around super-fast or seeing how quickly it is for sunrise to turn into sunset in a matter of seconds. So, if you are wondering what that is and how you can go about recording it, a time-lapse video is a type of photography/videography technique.

It looks impressive, but it's pretty simple and requires minimal skills to do it. Apple built this feature right into the iPhone 11 Pro and Pro Max. By capturing footages at selected intervals to create a time-lapse video of an experience over a period of time, time-lapse videos are able to make it possible to use them in situations when one wants to create a short, memorable moments by combining still pictures or for situations where the sun is on its way to set or a flowing traffic.

To shoot time-lapse videos on your iPhone 11 Pro or iPhone 11 Pro Max with ultra-wide and telephoto lenses, you open the Camera app on your iPhone. Then, set up your iPhone where you want to capture a scene in motion. By swiping on the viewfinder from left to right, you can activate the time-lapse mode when the phone is in Portrait orientation or top to bottom when it is instead in a landscape position.

To use the ultra-wide lens for a time-lapse video, you tap the ".5" button next to "Time-Lapse," if what you want to do is zoom in, tap 2x. You can use the front-facing camera for time-lapse videos, but you won't be able to change the zoom. Tap the record button, and it will start recording. Tap it again when you're done. A clock-like animation spin will appear around the record button. For each revolution made, 1 second worth of video would have been recorded. This is mostly a result of the fact that time-lapse makes a video recording to be sped up by a considerable amount of time, so to put together a scene that's only a few seconds long, you would have to have it recorded for much longer than that.

Recording and Editing a Slow-motion Video

If you record a slow-motion video, your video is recorded normally, but the slow-motion effect is only seen when the video is played back. You can choose the timing of your video by just editing it to achieve what you want.

To turn on the slow-motion feature, select Slo-mo mode. Then, press the Red Record button or any of the side volume buttons to start recording, tap to stop recording yet again. As stated earlier, you can also snap a still photo while recording. Tap the video thumbnail and then tap the Edit to set a portion of the video to play in slow motion and the rest at regular speed. Slide the vertical bars under the frame viewer to describe the slow-motion part you want to playback.

On your iPhone 11 Pro and iPhone 11 Pro Max, Slo-mo can be recorded with the front-facing camera by tapping the record button. To playback your slow-motion video, head to Photos app. Launch the Photos app, then scroll to the slow-motion video clip you want to speed up, to convert your low motion video clip into a regular video. There is a slider at the bottom of the screen showing where your video changes from steady speed to slow motion and vice versa. Drag the small white line on the left across the slider until all of the slow-motion areas become changed to their regular speed. You can adjust all of the slow-motion areas to regular speed or just a portion by moving the slider in either direction. Tap Done when you are pleased with the results or Cancel to discard.

To change a regular video to slow motion, open iMovie, and tap the + icon to start a new project using your desired video. Tap Edit to open the edit page. When this opens, on the editing timeline, hold down on the part of the video, you want to slow down.

You can also slow down all or a portion of a video just like earlier stated. If you're going to slow down the entire video, drag your finger across the whole timeline until it is highlighted in yellow. At the bottom part of the screen, click the speed adjustment icon. After this, drag your slider icon to decide on the desired speed of your clip, starting from one-eighth to double the pre-set or present rate of the video. Tap play to view your video and tap Done when you are satisfied with the results.

You can also reduce or increase the speed of your video using a third-party app like "Slow Fast Motion Video Editor," which is available on the App Store. You can also slow down or speed up parts of your video using the Slow and Fast app. To do this, start by trimming your video into clips and then choose from -8x to +8x for each clip.

Note that you can't reduce the speed of your slo-mo video if it is already playing at one-eighth speed.

Setting Focus Point

When you launch your Camera app, it will begin to focus on the center of the scene automatically. But sometimes you want to focus on something else, and you ask yourself, how do I get the camera to focus there?

To set "Focus Point," tap where you want the camera to focus, and you'll see a yellow box appear. The box is a mark of your focus area, so keep tapping until you see it. You can stroll or check-up or down on the screen after setting the focus point to adjust the exposure. Swiping up brightens the scene and swiping down darkens it. Now, tap the shutter button as soon as you're done adjusting the focus and exposure to snap your photo.

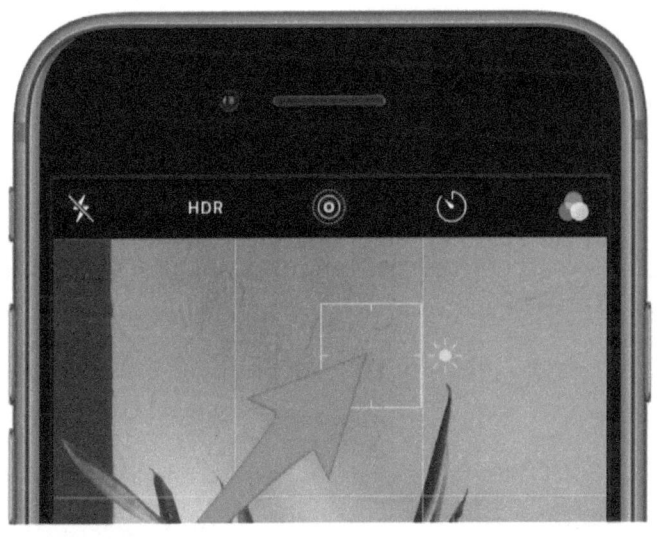

You can also adjust the Auto Exposure/Auto Focus Lock when you are dealing with a scene with a lot of movement, such as people walking around in the background. With AE/AF Lock, your focus point and exposure levels will ensure that the focus remains the same. Mobile apps, for example, like Halide or Camera+, allow you to turn off autofocus and do manual focus.

This provides you with a slider that will enable the individual the choice of adjustments to focus gradually. It is more subtle, but if you watch the scene while you move the focus slider, different parts come into focus. You can have it stopped by adjusting the focus when the scene is just how you like it and snap your photo. By tapping the app's Autofocus button, the manual focus can be changed.

Switching Between the Wide, Ultra-Wide and Telephoto Lenses

Apple, by creating an Ultra-Wide lens, has made it possible to create wonderful pictures on our smartphone. This new Ultra-Wide camera lens helps to capture a wide range of scenes, and it has brought a whole lot of opportunities to smart photography. While you may feel switching cameras is not easy, Apple has made it very easy to switch quickly. At the lower part of the viewfinder, you will see three buttons slated: 0.5x, 1x, and 2x. Tap the 0.5x for Ultra-Wide, 1x (default) for Wide, and 2x for Telephoto as you wish.

You can also tap and hold the camera selection buttons to change to the zoom dial wheel, and finally, manually adjust how far or near you want your subject to be in.

The Wide-angle Camera is the standard camera, and it is useful for shooting as fast as possible. As the name suggests, the Wide-angle camera has a wide field of view that captures a wide range. This is used for landscapes, still life, group photos, and even street photography.

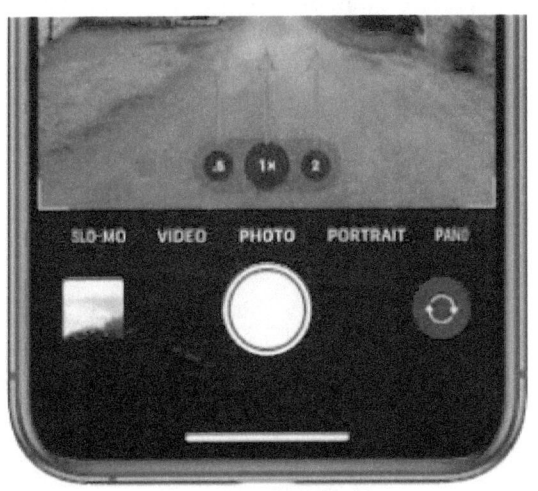

You should use the Wide-angle and Burst mode when capturing action shots. If there are images outside the picture frame that you want to include, you can use the Ultra-Wide. The Ultra-Wide lens capture areas which the wide-angle cannot take.

Note that you need to click on Photos Capture Outside the Frame and Videos Capture Outside the Frame in the Settings to have this option enabled and use it to your advantage. However, doing this also requires your photo format to be High Efficiency (HEIC), which is an image format that uses advanced compression for high-quality files in smaller sizes, so it is impossible to do this if you prefer JPEG.

High Dynamic Range Imaging (HDR)

The HDR can help you take better-looking photos by providing a better dynamic range to the images. The dynamic range for every image is the ratio of light to dark, so with HDR on, rather than take only one photo, HDR utilizes three photos, taken at multiple exposures.

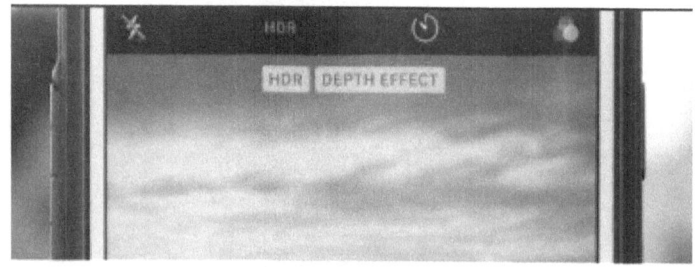

You're then able to, at that point, use a picture editing program to put those three pictures together and highlight the most beautiful parts of each photo. HDR in Camera enables you to get excellent shots in high-contrast circumstances. At different exposures, the iPhone takes multiple pictures in rapid succession and combines them to add more highlight and shadow detail to your images.

By default, when it's most effective, iPhone will automatically use HDR. However, if you want to activate this feature manually, you can do the following; go to

Settings -> Camera, switch off Smart HDR, then tap HDR to toggle it off or on from the camera screen.

If your image looks a bit too dark, which often happens if your setting has too much backlight, HDR can help brighten the foreground without washing out your photo's well-lit segments. More often, large scene photos have a lot of contrast between the sky and the ground, which is challenging for your camera to accommodate in just one frame, using HDR, you can catch the color of the sky without making the atmosphere appear too dark. Lighting is one of a good photo's most essential aspects, but too much lighting on someone's face like intense sunlight can trigger dark shadows, bright glare, and other unflattering features that HDR can even out and make your subject look better.

How to Select Camera Aspect Ratio

You may need to change the aspect ratio of an image, so it is compatible with the device you are using.

The introduction of different aspect ratio shooting modes is a particular change in the iPhone 11 Pro and the iPhone 11 Pro Max Camera app.

Previous versions of the iPhone had Camera apps that only offered a single 1:1 aspect ratio shooting mode referred to as the Square. The iPhone 11 Pro and Pro

Max also have the advantage that it allows users to select different ratios later in the editing mode of the Photos app, however, users are allowed to choose between three aspect ratio options while shooting in the Camera app from 1:1, 4:3 and 16:9.

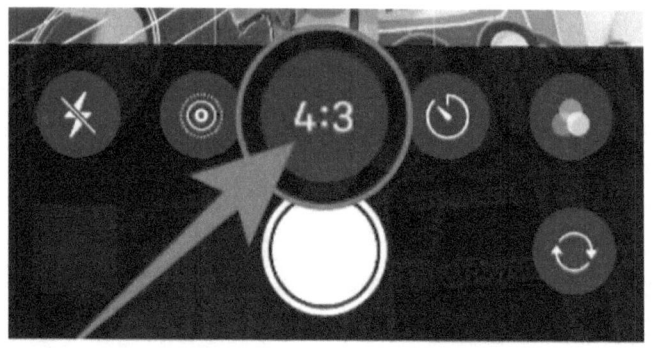

The 1:1 aspect ratio, as stated earlier, is a square. The very first number indicates the width, while the second number indicates the height. The 4:3 aspect ratio means that for every 4 inches of width in an image, you will have 3 inches of height. The 16:9 aspect ratio helps create wide or large images like a cover image on social media.

To get to the different shooting modes, open the Camera app, then tap the chevron (the arrow in the middle of the screen when in the camera) at the top of the viewfinder (or to the side of it, in landscape shooting) to reveal the hidden drawer. In the test that is directly below or to the side of the viewfinder, select the most preferred aspect ratio from the expanded 4:3 button menu and snap your shot. You can re-crop the 1:1 and 16:9 ratios in your edit if you want.

Take Portrait mode photos

Portrait mode on your iPhone 11 Pro and Pro Max camera can help you apply a depth of field effect to keep your subjects sharp while the background is blurred. It is handy when taking pictures of pets, people, and objects.

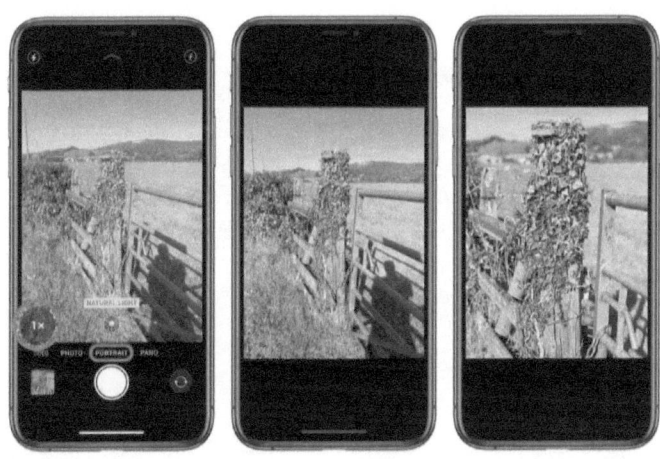

You can also use your portrait mode on the front-facing TrueDepth camera to take selfies, and in both cases, you can apply and adjust different lighting effects to your portrait mode photos.

Taking Portrait Mode Photos

On iPhone 11 Pro and Pro Max can apply lighting effects to your Portrait mode pictures that are of studio quality. To do this, you;

- Select Portrait mode at the bottom of the camera app
- Follow the onscreen tips in ensuring that your subject is framed in the yellow portrait box.
- To choose a lighting effect for your Portrait Mode, you drag the boxlike symbol ⬡ on the area you want to focus on.

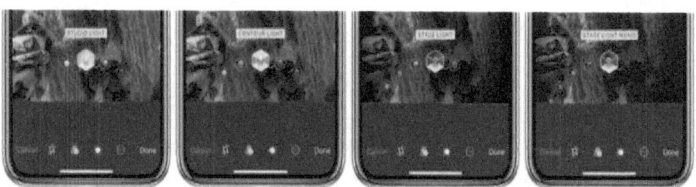

- With a lighting effect selected, you can now tap the Shutter button to take the shot.

The available lighting options include:

Natural Light: This places the subject to be in sharp focus against a blurred background.

Studio Light: This places the subject to be brightly lit and creates an overall clean look for the photos.

Contour Light: This places the subject to have dramatic shadows in the presence of highlights and lowlights.

Stage Light: This places the subject to be spot lit against a deep black background.

Stage Light Mono: This has a similar effect as the Stage Light except that the photo will be in classic black and white.

High-Key Light Mono: This lighting effect is used to create grayscale subjects on white backgrounds

You can then turn off the portrait mode when you are through with using the Portrait mode effect in Photographs. To do this, tap to open the photo, select Edit, and then tap Portrait to turn it on or off.

Adjusting Portrait Mode's Lighting Effects

On your iPhone 11 Pro and Pro Max, the position and intensity of each Portrait Lighting effect can be adjusted to sharpen the eye area or to make the facial features bright and smooth.

- Select Portrait mode from the options below the viewfinder, then frame your subject.

- Next, you tap at the top of the screen to activate the Portrait Lighting slider.

- Then you drag the slider that appears below the frame to either the right or left position and observe the effect.

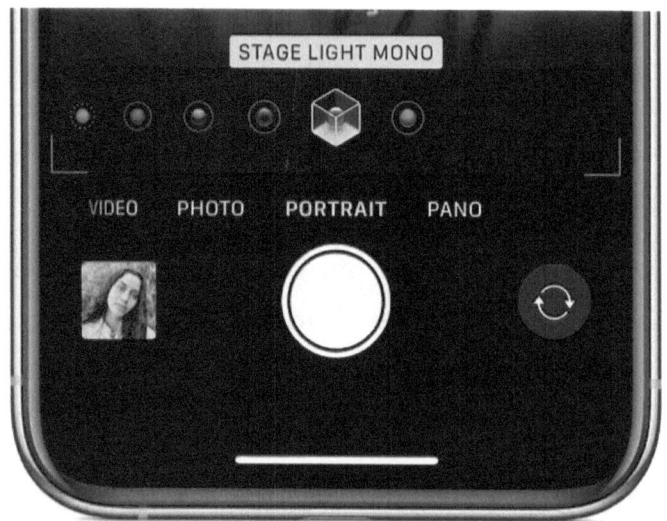

- Once satisfied, you now tap the Shutter button to take the shot.

- Even after previously taking a photo in Portrait mode without adding the lighting effect or you are unsatisfied with the lighting effect applied, you can still open Photos and use the Portrait Lighting slider to adjust the lighting effect further.

Adjusting Depth Control in Portrait Mode

On the iPhone 11 Pro and Pro Max, you can decide by how much you want the background to be blurred by using the Depth Control slider to adjust the level of blur in the background of your Portrait mode photos.

The way to do that is to;

- Once again, select Portrait mode and then frame your subject.

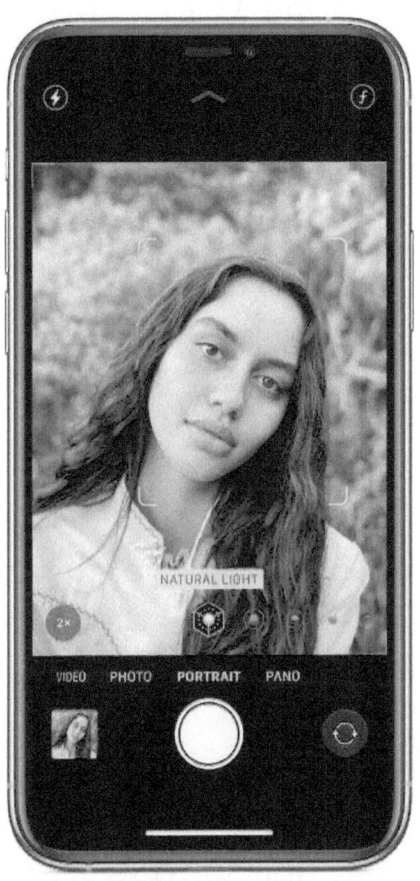

- Next, you tap 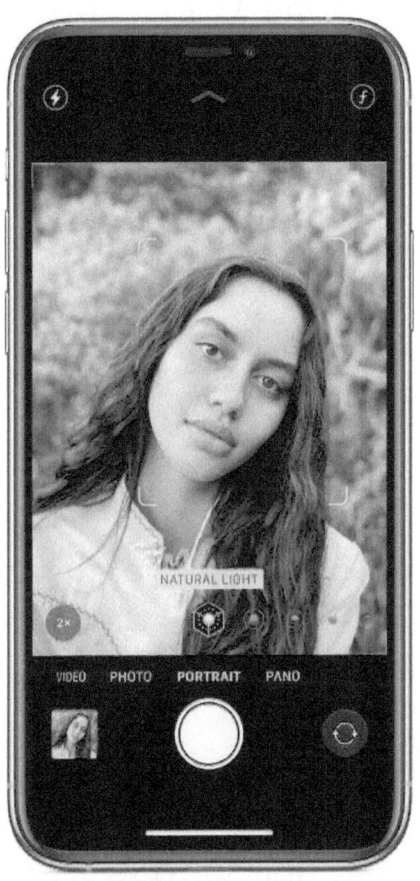 located at the top-right corner of the screen to display the Depth Control slider.

- Then you drag the slider that appears below the frame either to the right or left to have the effect changed.

- You can now tap the Shutter button to take the shot.

Filters on iPhone 11 Pro and Pro Max

The filters that come with the iPhone 11 Pro and Pro Max can make the phone a more exciting and fun way to enhance the appearance of a photo.

Anyone accustomed to using filters knows that no matter how well the iPhone 11 Pro and Pro Max does its job of photography, you will sometimes want to use the features of the filter included on the iPhone to make your pictures have a different feel from the norm.

For those who are already used to filters on previous versions of the iPhone and have recently upgraded to the iPhone 11 Pro and Pro Max, but have given up on ever making use of filters because it seems to be missing, well, the good news is that it is not one of those features like 3D Touch that was removed from this version, instead, Apple chose to relocate it to another part of the phone different from where many previous iPhone users may have been used to.

Because of how Apple has redesigned the UI of the iPhone 11 Pro and Pro Max to be able to accommodate more features like the QuickTake video, Night mode, and others, Apple had to move it from the top-right corner within the camera app where it used to be to a new location which we will talk about shortly.

How to Use Filters

To easily access the filters on your camera app, follow the steps outlined below:

- Tap the Camera app to have it opened
- Next, you tap on the arrow icon at the top of the screen to expose additional controls below the viewfinder, just above the shutter icon.
- There you will find the filter icon at the extreme right, next to the timer mode option.
- To continue, next, you tap on the "group of circles" icon.
- Here, you will now be able to access the filters available on the iPhone 11 Pro and Pro Max.
- Select any of the options you want and apply it on the picture

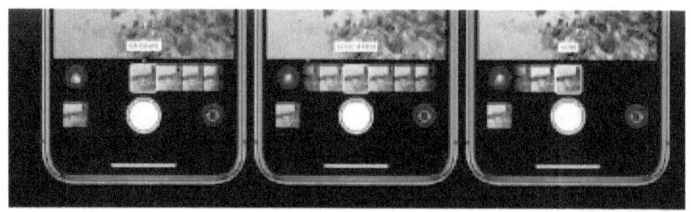

Live rendering Feature of iPhone 11 Pro and Pro Max for Bokeh and HDR

The iPhone 11 Pro and Pro Max have been able to take advantage of improved processing power that comes with the new iPhone to be able to provide an increased real-time rendering of more correct photo effects, including bokeh and HDR. This is one area where the new iPhone outpaces previous models of the iPhone as well as other competitor flagship phones.

What now makes the iPhone 11 Pro and Pro Max stand out is that, instead of the usual situation where you had to first capture an image before looking at the result to see how well the effect had turned out, on the iPhone 11 Pro and Pro Max, a real-time simulation of the photos as it is being composed will make it easier to ensure that the photo comes out the way you want it to.

Chapter 6

Different Ways of Using The iPhone 11 Pro and Pro Max Camera App

Zooming on your Camera App

- Open the Camera app on your iPhone.

- Tap "0.5x, 1, or 2" to change between the cameras depending on the view you prefer or want to capture.

- Hold down the camera selection buttons until the zoom dial appears.

- Then, drag the zoom dial back and forth to smoothly transition between the wide, ultra-wide, and telephoto cameras and their digital zoom levels.

Recording When in Photo Mode

- When you long-press the "Shutter button" in photo mode, video recording by default begins, but removing your finger will cause the video to stop recording.

- Swiping the recording button to the "Lock icon" on the right keeps your recording going even when you lift your finger from your iPhone.

Taking Burst Pictures

- Press and swipe the "Shutter button" to the left (quickly so you don't start a quick video recording).

- Lift your finger the "Shutter button" to stop taking your burst photo.

Accessing Hidden Camera Controls

- Swipe up the "Viewfinder" or tap the "Arrow" at the top of the screen to expose a new control panel just above the shutter button.

Setting the Camera App Flash

- Open the hidden camera controls
- Tap the "Flash" button
- Select either "Auto, On or Off."

Setting the Night Mode of the Camera

- Open the hidden camera controls
- Tap to choose the night mode
- Slide the Night mode dial in the left or right direction to determine the length of time it would take for the night mode to capture an image or to turn the night mode off.

Taking Live Photos

- Open the hidden camera controls

- Tap "Auto, On or Off" to take live photos when you tap the "Live photos" button.

Setting the Aspect Ratio of Camera

- Open the hidden camera controls
- Tap the "Aspect ratio" button to select an aspect ratio you want to use, either "Square (1:1), 4:3 or 16:9."

Setting Camera Timer for Self-Picture

- Tap the "Timer button" to set the time range within which you want your photos to be captured (3s or 10s or turn the timer off).

Adding Filters to your Photos

- Filters can also be added to your photos using the "Filter button."

Editing your Photos

- To edit your photo, open the "Photos" app on your iPhone
- Tap the picture you want to work on.
- And then tap the "Edit" button.

Cropping your Photos

- Tap the "Crop" button to crop the picture to the required size, pinch in on the image to zoom out as much of the ultra-wide view as you want.
- And then tap "Done."

Manually Switching from Close to Wide-Angle Selfies

- Tap the "Perspective flip" button to activate the front-facing camera
- Then tap the "Arrows button" to manually switch between close and wide-angle selfies.

Automatically Switching from Close to Wide-Angle Selfies

- Rotate your iPhone to one side to automatically switch to wide-angle selfies.

Taking a Slo-Mo Recording

- Open the camera app
- Swipe the "Mode dial" to the right until you're on slo-mo
- Tap to select it and you can start taking your slo-mo pictures

Locking the Camera App Aperture

- Also, using your iPhone camera to achieve a perfect image focus, you can do so by pressing and holding on to the subject until you see the yellow AE / AF Lock warning. This means that the automatic exposure metering and automatic focus metering has been locked on your subject. This makes the subject sharper, clearer, and more enhanced.

- If you are trying to shoot macro photography or want to prevent your iPhone camera from trying to capture a different subject in the picture, this can be incredibly useful to lock your focus point on your current subject and avoid distractions.
- Adjusting the yellow exposure tool helps to correct any underexposed or overexposed image.
- Tap the focus square and exposure slider once
- Then, using the sun icon to raise your exposure by sliding upwards or through exposure by moving the slides downwards.

Unlocking the Camera App Aperture

- To remove the lock, tap anywhere else on the frame, this automatically removes the lock.

Finally, the iPhone 11, iPhone 11 Pro, or 11 Pro Max has stellar cameras that bring you enhanced zoom capabilities, a new feature called Deep Fusion, and a new night mode for taking photos in dark environments, which you can decide to switch off or not.

Chapter 7

Useful Third-Party Apps For iPhone 11 Pro and Pro Max

There are a lot of third-party apps you can use to support your iPhone 11 Pro or Pro Max built-in Camera to have enhanced camera output or better-quality photos. Most of these apps may require some monthly charges or annual subscription to unlock all or a few features in them and for productive use. Some of the common apps include:

Halide

For anyone that desires a camera app that gives the user control over certain camera functions like focus, aperture and exposure, then Halide will suit your need. If you have some photography knowledge and experience, you will love this app, as it allows you to create perfect photos by being exact with how you set your various parameters, including how you control everything from shutter speed to ISO.

In addition to taking advantage of the iPhone 11 Pro and Pro Max depth features, it also allows images to be taken with the smart RAW for quality pictures. You will also like how quick it is, which can make a difference when you're trying to capture the right shot.

It also gives you full control over the picture you take and provides detailed information on how the camera is processing the data and the settings.

There is a fantastic portrait mode camera that has support for TrueDepth camera for your selfies, including an AR mode that is nifty to see the images as they stretch out into 3D space. It is designed for you to have various options while retaining the ease of using it with one hand. It is an app for those who are used to taking photos with their phone and an excellent step up from Apple's default camera app.

ProCamera

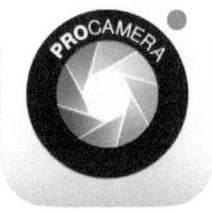

This is an iOS photo, video, and editing app bursting with the most modern technology. It is considered one of the best of iPhone's Camera app. Its interface is similar to a DSLR control that suits everyone since you can shoot in automatic mode, semi-auto mode or fully manual mode. The procamera is more concerned about giving you the maximum control before you take the shot. With this app, you are better equipped to change the setting on the app just as easily as you would be able to do with a DSLR including settings like ISO, shutter speed, and white balance which can affect your output image generally.

The procamera's interface isn't that different from iPhone Camera app, but its focus is more on controlling shots than on extras things like Panorama, Time Lapse, and Slo-Mo. It creates an Exposure Value (EV) slider from the screen bottom-up, which is excellent for shots, and the camera has set this lightness or darkness for what you want to show in the image, often used when the subject has a bright background behind it.

Focus

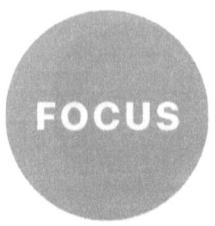

If you love the iPhone's Portrait Mode, you are also likely to love Focus. This app will allow you to go back and adjust focus after you have taken a photo. The app allows for more advanced depth map editing, changing foreground and background separately. A new update to focus lets you turn any photo into a portrait mode style image with a fully adjustable depth of field.

Focus bring DSLR-like photography to your iPhone with a big aperture and depth of field (bokeh effect). Portrait photo with a depth of field allows you to direct your focus after shooting. With the lighting tool, checking of portrait picture in true 3D space, adding of lights and adjusting colors and brightness are now all possible. It is more powerful and flexible than portrait lighting, which Apple videos does.

Adobe Lightroom

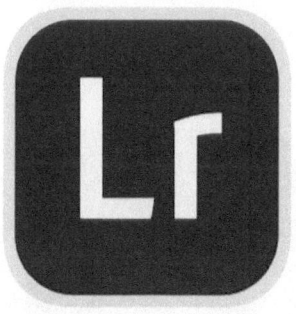

This app supports HDR capture mode for your iPhone 11 Pro and iPhone 11 Max. The new version of Lightroom is one of the most fantastic photo management and editing tool you should get on your iPhone and with its amazing features, and you will surely need this app.

With its built-in camera, a subscription to Adobe Creative Cloud means you can store your photo library on their server, and you get to edit photos on the go with the same powerful tools you have on your desktop. Lightroom with your phone photography helps you capture and edit photos to create stunning images. With convenient editing tools like sliders, or filters for pictures, Lightroom makes photo editing simple. This helps for importing and saving your images, viewing and strategically organizing, hashtagging, editing, and sharing large numbers of images.

LumaFusion

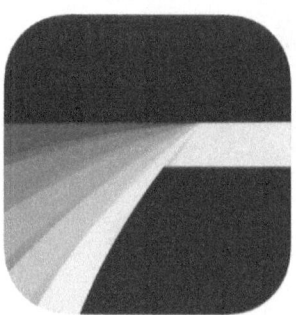

LumaFusion is a popular app among producers, mobile journalists, filmmakers, and professional video makers who see it as a powerful multi-track video editor for telling compelling video stories. If you want to edit videos with a grade A software, LumaFusion is the best you're going to get on iOS. The power of the A13 chip on both the iPhone 11 Pro and Pro Max makes editing even 4K video fast and straightforward.

This allows you to import videos from your device storage as well as every popular cloud service (Dropbox, Google Drive, One Drive) or on shared network drives.

Obscura

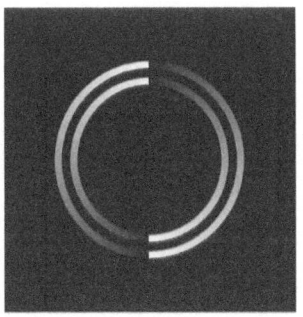

Obscura has a varied kind of controls which you would generally expect from a proper DSLR to your iPhone. Designed with easy to use and flexible controls, ergonomic design and beautiful filters, Obscura is the Camera app that gets out of your way. Despite its simplicity, it's quite powerful. It consists of the Control Wheel, Powerful Library Tools, and Quick Adjustments.

Obscura's innovative Control Wheel allows you to scroll between different camera options with ease. It is very comfortable to use in both portrait and landscape modes, and even lefties are not left out because the app also makes provision for them alongside righties.

Obscura's library lets you see your full photo library, as well as open specific albums. Not only can you go through your pictures, but you are also able to edit and even view picture details. The app allows you quickly and easily adjust focus, exposure compensation, ISO and shutter speed.

VSCO

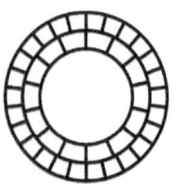

VSCO

VSCO possesses many filters and editing features, but you will need an annual subscription to unlock all these features to create beautiful images. VSCO applies a combination of effects, filters, and editing tools to make it easy and fun to apply creative effects to your photos. This app consists of many image manipulation tools that include features like exposure, skewing, brightness, contrast, clarity, straightening, skin tones, temperature, vignette, and a wide range of exciting features. While VSCO focuses on the post-shot editing experience, its built-in camera has many capabilities.

With VSCO, you can change your image focus, white balance, ISO, shutter speed, and how your image can be lit up. This app allows you to use your iPhones 11 Pro and Pro Max to shoot in RAW also.

VSCO is a free download, but you only get a handful of filters in the free version. VSCO X gives you access to all of VSCO's filters and tools.

Cam 5

Cam 5 offers fine-grained control and features typically found in DSLRs, but the interface never gets old fashioned or complicated to use. You get all the features and modes you would expect an app like that to have. It contains ability to adjust exposure, shutter priority, ISO priority, HDR. That is not all, it is also suitable for several extended exposure modes, timers for shutter, and other applicable photographic formats. Many Cam 5's features are easily accessible from the main interface and not hidden.

Pixlr

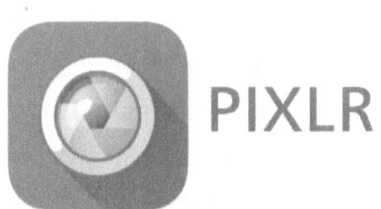

This app allows you to experience smarter and faster photo editing tools. It is one of the available photo editor apps needed for quick yet savvy edits and comes equipped with just the right amount of easy to navigate photo editing tools.

Many photo editors today have a social platform built into them, even though you can use them as offline apps with a plethora of photo editing tools. Pixlr contains similar tools as you would find on some other mobile photo editing tools, even then, it makes room for many different possible forms of adjustments you can make with it.

Pixlr has about two million combinations that you can choose from, options if selected, can make your photos a lot more beautiful. Errors are pretty much common in many photos, fortunately, with Pixlr you are able to edit pictures to a desired level. It comes with features like the ability to have blemishes and red-eye removed, and an ability to have teeth whitened with its relatively simple and easy-to-use tools.

Adobe Photoshop Express

Adobe Photoshop Express is another excellent choice app to have among the third-party apps. It has a lot of unique tools in it to make manipulating photos more attractive. One of the features allows you to create a photo assemblage in just a few seconds, and you will have an array of pictures arranged according to your preference. This can be used primarily as a sort-of memory board.

Photoshop Express can store photos in tons of different file formats. With this feature, the phone images can be manipulated as well as any photos from DSLRs and others. It has a varying level of supported features.

Vintique

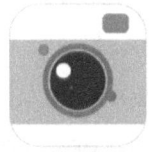

Vintique is useful to apply vintage effects to your photos and videos. The app applies effects in real-time for photos and videos, giving you your desired output, what you edited is what you will get. Also, you can further tweak the contrast, saturation, temperature, exposure and other settings slightly to get the expected results on your iPhone 11 Pro and Pro Max. It contains more than 100 filters that can be used to add texture, flare effects and frames in whichever way you want.

Boomerang

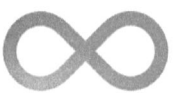

Boomerang allows you to create mini videos with a back and forth loop effect, which you might prefer. The app captures ten photos in a row, stitches them together and even removes any shakes or moves or inebriates loss of focus from the final video. There is no sign-up required, unlike other video apps, you can also create videos using the primary or the front camera. The app saves all videos you shoot with the app automatically to your iPhone 11 Pro or Pro Max memory.

Fyuse

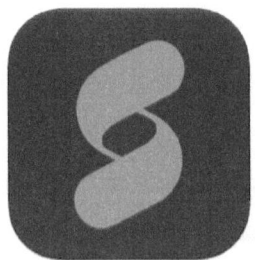

The concept behind this app is that it enables you to capture 3D photos of any subject in any way you want. The app demands that you capture the subject from different angles and include other details from your phone's accelerometer, the app sticks the pictures together to create a 360-degree 3D photo. The app allows you to tilt your screen to move around to view the images from whichever way you would prefer. It also has its social network so that you can share your photos or view others, and this is subject to your choice of either sharing or not. It is truly a fun app to have.

LiveBlend

This app can be used by iOS supported smartphones. This app is the only one available that lets you create double exposure photos in real-time.

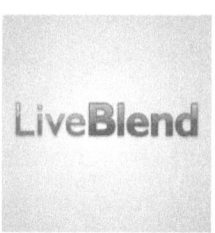

By selecting a picture from your gallery, the app automatically uses your phone camera's feed to display an overlaid double exposure result. The app allows you to capture and create a double exposure video in full High definition resolution.

If you prefer to use existing photos for double exposure, you can check out apps like Fused and Instant Blend, and these apps are also reviewed.

Horizon Camera

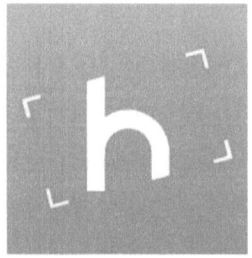

The app allows you to create a mix of horizontal and vertical videos when you rotate your phone. Horizon allows your phone to record videos and take photos in landscape no matter how or the direction the phone is held.

You can also use this app whenever you want to auto-level your videos so that they appear parallel to the ground. The app has support for up to 4k video recording and can be used for recording slow-motion.

Paper Camera

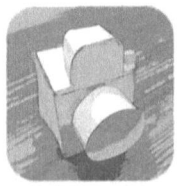

This app shows you varying cartoon effects in real-time on your smartphone from your phone's camera feed. You can check through various effects in real-time, including sketches, comic-books, halftone, noir, and many more.

There is another option that allows you to change the brightness, edges, strokes manually as much as you desire. While the app is free for iOS, there will be a watermark placed on all images, this app demands you to pay a certain fee to remove it, a fee for added control and also an amount to allow you to import videos into the app rather than capture through the app.

Candy Camera

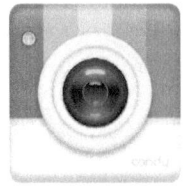

If you are a selfie enthusiast, then this app Candy Camera is quite a recommended app. Included in it is a silent camera mode that enables you take selfies without the noise you have come to associate with the shutter which allows for privacy.

Also, the app offers a handy function that you can improve your selfies with, a collage mode for displaying photos, and the ability to apply stickers as you want. This exclusive iOS app gives you an advance control to add depth of field as well as a bokeh effect on your photos. This app has an easy-to-use 'tap to focus' system that works surprisingly well, giving you a focused image. Moreover, there is also an option to mask or erase a particular object from the photo with the opportunity to auto-detect edges to keep things simple and straightforward. You can even adjust the level of blur, highlights and overall effect to suit your taste and give you the desired image.

Enlight

This app can be used by iOS supported smartphones. If there were ever an all-in-one editing app, you could get for your iOS, this would be precisely what you need for your iPhone 11 Pro and Pro Max. The app records a sheer number of filters, effects and tools.

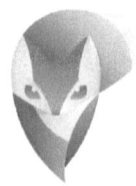

Enlight gives you a fantastic picture. This app gives you a camera roll so that you can choose images to edit. The toolbar is always visible and can be moved to increase the workspace you wish to have. You can choose to edit, adjusts, crop, skew, refit, change clarity, add filters, remove objects, heal patch postures, add text, decals, convert to the meme, make collages, modify for Instagram, and other handful uses for your iPhone 11 Pro and Pro Max. Once done, you can share from the app to whatever social media page you desire.

The app allows you to choose your output quality (even PNG, TIFF), and some tutorials help you find your way around the features such as masks, gradients and double exposure which might be complicating.

Snapwire

SnapWire videos a list of paid photo requests from various brands. You can submit existing photos or capture a new one of your choice.

Snapwire

If your photo is nominated, you get points, and also get paid. You can even create your photo portfolio on the app for interested parties to view and purchase your captivating photos. This is an exciting way to earn on your iPhone 11. There are photo requests that can pay as high as $1, 000.

Editing Photos with New Designs

While it is true that your iPhone 11 Pro and Pro Max 11 cam make taking amazing pictures more natural, it won't always get you your desired effect, in such cases, you will need to make use of photo editing apps to improve on the quality of your photos. Some of these photo editing apps can enhance the quality of your photographs and to produce pictures with a more fantastic and better effect. Some of these apps are listed below:

Snapseed

Snapseed is regarded by many as the top phone app for editing photos and achieving a crisp output. The app is one of the most resourceful editing apps you can use on your iPhone 11 Pro and Pro Max. It allows you to adjust an image's color balance, saturation, curves, and sharpness, etc. It also allows you to create "presets" and save them for future references. With Snapseed, you can edit your snapshots in a snap. The app offers a wide range of features and is not difficult to use. With its intuitive interface, editing your photos will be a fun experience as it should be.

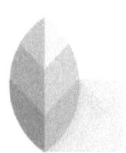

This tool allows you adjust how sharp, the curves, saturation and color balance of your photos. For those who often post on Instagram, this is the one app for your pictures you would want to have especially since you can create presets which you can save and use again. Using this approach, your Instagram feed can have the same theme and maintain consistency.

VSCO

This app allows you to add filters to your images and make slight changes to contrast, brightness, color balance, as well as making photos sharp. When through, you can save your pictures to share. VSCO app prides itself in its versatility and its ability to change its contrasts, color balance, sharpness, and brightness of your pictures to achieve your desired result.

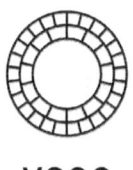

VSCO

You can be sure if you ever get stuck at anything you will be able to find many creative tutorials and community stories that can serve as a useful source of inspiration and you will surely find your way through.

Hyperspektiv

This is an app that can be used to create a cover image for your SoundCloud upload as the features allow this.

Using the app's many filters, you can edit your images to entirely unrecognizable forms. It will enable you to create "trippy" pictures and videos with a simple swipe of your fingers. This is for sure, not your ordinary photo editing app, as it comes with a lot of complicated but modern features.

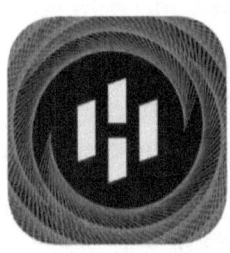

What makes this app so different is that it offers a wide range of filters that you can use to make extreme changes to your photos as you desire that can be so drastic that you might not even be able to recognize your photos after you are done experimenting and trying out these features.

Adobe Lightroom CC

It is a tested and trusted member of the Adobe suite. Adobe Lightroom CC allows you to shoot RAW photos in HDR mode and automatically organizes them in the cloud's gallery so as not to consume the phone's space. Lightroom is also a great app to tweak your photographs.

Some of these tweaks are HSL Sliders for bringing out the blue skies with one hidden slider. There is also the Sharpening Preview, which is used to selectively sharpen the edges in your photo and the Boundary Warp which is used to stretch your panoramas to avoid cropping.

Instagram

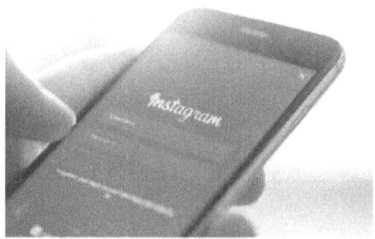

Although many people will be surprised to find Instagram here, considering it is supposed to be a social media app, Instagram, as far as photo editing app is concerned, is one of the few best photo editing apps which it offers as part of its photo-sharing features.

Its array of editing tools is relatively simple and easy to use, and once you log in, you will be granted access to all sorts of tools like saturation adjustments, filters, cropping, and many more features. When you snap your picture with the Instagram camera or pick one out of your gallery, you can then use Instagram's built-in functions to edit your photo and, finally, share it with your Instagram page or Story on your iPhone 11 Pro or Pro Max.

FilterStorm Neue

FilterStorm Neue has all the photo editing tools you will need on an iPhone, especially on your iPhone Pro and Pro Max. It offers a variety of features for both beginners and experts in making their pictures look astonishing and remarkable. It provides advanced masking tools that include histogram range and smart brush to clean up your photos and make them look savvy.

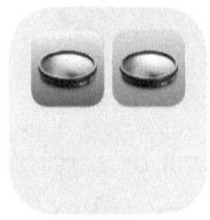

It also has a lot of blend modes, that includes saturation, luminosity, and color dodge, which enables you to improve on your picture quality. This allows you to be able to edit your iPhone 11 Pro and Pro Max pictures in full size, it also enables you to edit all the small details. The 10-step undo history feature allows you to see all the changes you have made so far and assist in retracing your steps if necessary.

It has a wide range of advantages that are perfect for quick editing. Even though many beginners find it suitable for their use, many experts are still able to make the most out of it. The only disadvantage you may experience is that the masking feature is not as good as some of its competitors in the market.

Affinity Photo

If you are not interested in signing up for an Adobe suite subscription at all, the Affinity Photo app is a way to go around it. Created by Serif Labs, it is for sure one of the most powerful photo editing apps available in the app market, and even though it has a steep learning curve.

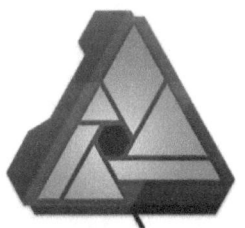

You can use the money saved to invest in lenses for your iPhone and create stunning shots with the app, and the lenses are also quite crucial for your iPhone 11 Pro and Pro Max. It comes with functions like contrast push, panorama stitching, RAW editing, digital painting, batch processing, and focus stacking. The performance and power that this photo editing app is able to deliver is capable of blowing you away through the quality of amazing and beautiful pictures it is able to create.

Enlight Photofox

Enlight Photofox is an app that helps give your pictures an artistic effect by combining photo editing tools with other innovative tools that help in transforming your photos into astonishing photos.

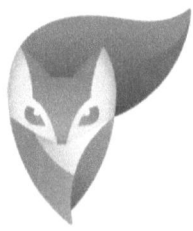

You can use this app to merge up to 5 layers different to form one composition. You can also edit each layer separately in whatever way you want. It also has traditional darkroom feature that allow for adjusting of tones, contrasts, and other details of your photos and making them sharper, clearer and crisp. Your photos can be made to look colorful with the Light Fix feature that lets you add an array of light flares and leaks to your photos, making it brighter. The lighting of your camera can be increased or decreased, and even the opacity can be changed. The app also offers features such as effects, presets, filters, etc. The app is compatible with 16-bit and raw images, however, the app has a bit of a learning curve.

Pixelmator

If you are already familiar with the Pixelmator on the MacOS app, then the Pixelmator will need no introduction except to know that the Pixelmator on the iOS has many fascinating photo editing tools suitable that can expand the capabilities of your iPhone 11 Pro and Pro Max that can make your photos look sharper, savvier, and more classic. With advanced photo editing tools, this app helps you blur imperfections, control your picture tone and also the gradient of your photos by adding different effects.

The painting feature of the app allows you to draw and paint anything you want over your photos as you desire. Painting in layers helps make your photos look more realistic, add text, effects, and customized shapes to bring your photos to life and make them more real. Using the precise selection tool that comes with this app to edit parts of the photo that needs to be improved. The app has an easy to use interface, but the app is costly for what it offers.

Mextures

Mextures allows you to take your photos to the next level by offering editing tools that make your photos look more artistic and edgy. You can make your photos anyway your want, in whatever way you desire from the over 150 textures you have to choose from. It comes with features that allow you to add unlimited layers to your photos and edit them as you go.

When such adjustments are made to these layer, it becomes easy to manage them while editing them especially in cases when you need to have them reviewed. The app comes with 30 film presets designed to make your photos stand out and be attractive. You can have your edits saved through the use of the app's Formula workflow, and this feature also works by allowing you to import other formulas uses and even share yours with other iPhone photographers like yourself. The app has several advantages, which include adding multiple layers of filters on a single photo and editing each anytime you want. You can also save your edits, share them and import other people's formulas to yours.

Fused

As the name suggests, this app lets you fuse or join two photos together to create a double exposure masterpiece. You can use the app for overlays on both images and videos, depending on your choice.

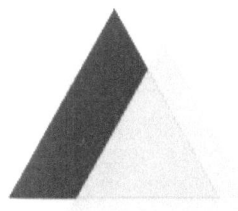

It has a blending mode that helps you merge the two photos you select seamlessly, also helps in masking effects, taking care of any imperfections in your overlay photo. The "Artists Collections" space allows you to view other user's amazing editing works and the processes involved. The Draw and Erase tools will enable you to enhance certain parts of your photos only. The app, like other apps, has an easy to use interface. The free version of the app offers quite some useful features.

The only detrimental factor about the app is that it has no "Undo" button, this means you can't go back a step in your editing process. You either have to get creative and edit over whatever you wanted to undo or start from scratch.

Canva

This is an app that gives you a creative graphic design template you might need. They are easy to use and have quite a handful of useful features, and templates for your iPhone 11 Pro and Pro Max demands.

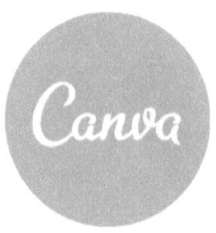

If you are someone that wants to create beautiful posters, cards, banners, and Instagram stories, then Canva is the answer to your requests. The app offers about 60,000 or more free templates you can choose from when starting a new graphic design project. You can upload and edit your photos as you add them to your design the way you choose. You can also choose from the list of preset illustrations present. Adding text to your photos is another necessary thing you could do, choosing from more than 700 font options with different formats. You can also change the color, size, and spacing of the font as well.

RAW Power

Expert iPhone photographers are going to enjoy editing raw images with this app, especially if this is done on their iPhone 11 Pro and Pro Max. RAW Power is a functional app that has undergone a lot of development due to its useful features.

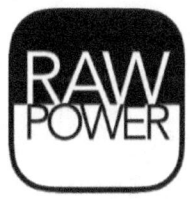

The features include using Apple's RAW decoder in editing your photos at your convenience, and you can zoom up to 800% to fine-tune little details in your image. This function is inbuilt in your iPhone 11 Pro and Pro Max. The app has a RAW contrast feature which allows you to adjust the sharpness and contrast of your image while preserving the details. It comes with features that enable you to crop, rotate, straighten, and flip images. For those who master how to use this app, they can always be assured of creating beautiful images. You can also apply the many presets the app offers to enhance your images. The app comes with various ways to make as many adjustments as you want without changing the pixels in the original picture and also has features for special RAW Images smart album to store all your edited photos for easy access. The app offers many exciting features, but the interface is way complicated.

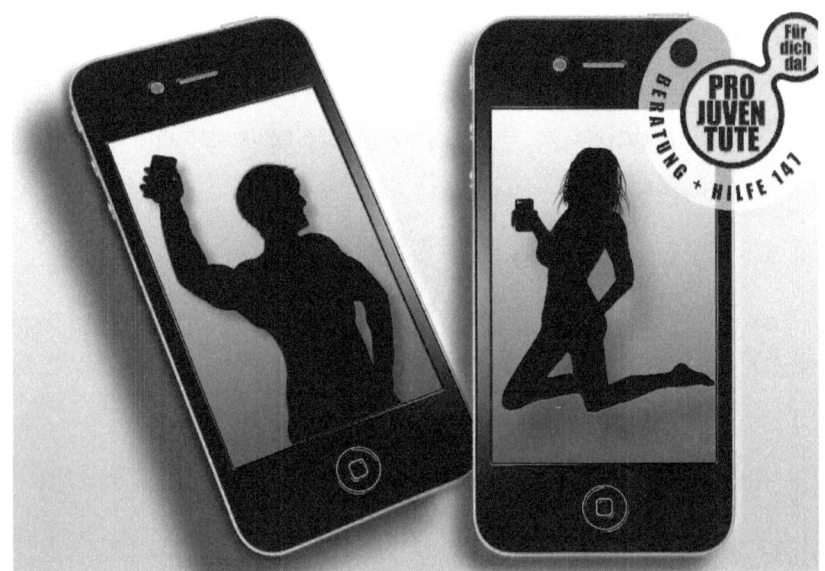

Chapter 8

Social Media Sharing

Photos can be shared on the iPhone iOS using the Smart sharing suggestions. Smart suggestions are a welcome addition to the iPhone 11 Pro and Pro Max. The first thing you notice when you want to share a photo is that there is now the inclusion of the features that assist in telling you who to share your images with, along with available AirDrop devices.

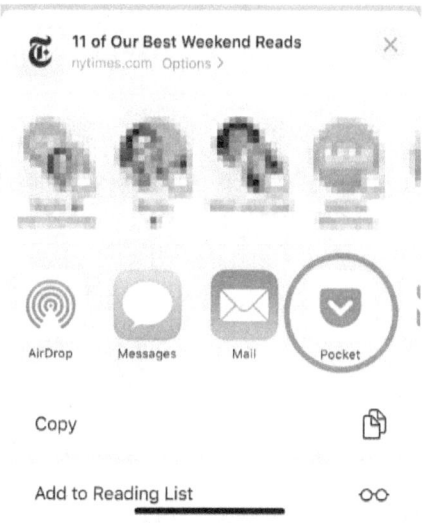

Before now, you were more likely to only see Message contacts show up as suggestions, but with time as third-party messaging apps like Snapchat, Facebook Messenger, or WhatsApp became updated with iOS 13 compatibility and their tips now also show up in the Share Sheet.

Also, below the contact and app suggestions, you will notice a long array of options in the Share Sheet. This list is made up of standard sharing options, including Copy. Other specific options will include adding a site to Bookmarks in Safari or setting a photo as wallpaper in Photo.

If you decide to install Apple's app shortcut, you will be exposed to a list of the applicable Shortcuts below the app-specific options. For example, if you have shortcuts that combine and edit photos, direct links to those shortcuts will now appear.

Photo Sharing Features on iPhone iOS

In earlier versions, you had to tap on the shortcut app icon, and then you select the shortcut from another list. By integrating the new Shortcuts in the Share Sheet, that first step is now removed, which, however, has the unintended effect of cluttering up the options for sharing.

You can edit and adjust whatever apps or options you want to be displayed in the Share list. For app suggestions, choose the edit button and select, but for the new sharing options, you need to scroll down to the bottom of the Share list and tap the "Edit Actions'. You will not be able to delete all of the action that show up, but you can add your frequently used to the Favorites list, putting them at the top and making them easier to find anytime you want to use them. You can also share multiple photos with an iCloud link.

These links remain available for 30 days and can be shared using certain apps. Photos and videos taken on your iPhone can also be shared with various Social Media apps like Twitter, Facebook, and Instagram.

Using the Share Sheet

To share photos or videos on your iPhone 11 Pro or iPhone 11 Pro Max, open the Photos app on your iPhone, then find the photo you wish to share. Click the "Share button" on your iPhone and then select the method with which you prefer to share the picture. There are three ways to share photos with your iPhone 11 Pro or iPhone 11 Pro Max. They include; Recent Contacts, Action Extensions, and App Extensions

The first row contains your contacts populated by your favorite contacts, and people recently contacted through Phone, Messages or FaceTime. With the Action extensions, you can use other app functions in Photos or do things like adding to a photo album or setting a photo as wallpaper. The third row (App extensions - colored app icons) allows you to share your photos directly with either Apple apps or third-party apps or Social Media like Twitter, and Instagram.

Conclusion

The iPhone 11 Pro and Pro Max Camera have the best triple-camera system compared to previous iPhones or other similar phones with the same number of cameras manufactured by other vendors. The three cameras at the back of the iPhone are for zooming straight out from the center. They capture the most true-to-life image with accurate colors and maintain sharpness across the image.

All of these can only happen if you master how to use the phone, which is what this book was written for. Knowing how to use the iPhone 11 Pro and Pro Max will help you know how to consistently generate the most realistic colors of images, you will know how to take advantage of the phone's night mode as well as other features that will show you how to come up with better photos, sharper details in your photos, improved tones, and contrast to preserve a scene's effects.

The book also shows you how balancing the light and dark areas can easily be done by you. You can now master the different lenses that come with the phone, including the 2x telephoto and how you can use it for portrait pictures.

Taking pictures that come out sharp, bright, and beautiful will become almost second nature to you because of your mastering of the different lenses of the iPhone 11 Pro and Pro Max. From reading this book, you learn how to set it manually, even achieving a bokeh effect.

Reading this book also opened you to the world of the video camera capabilities, as you get to practice more and more with the phone, you will find it to be the most exceptional video-recording experience you can ever enjoy on a phone. Your iPhone 11 Pro and Pro Max can handle changes in lighting, the switching of lenses, and stabilization far better than similar phones from other competitors that also have quadruple-lens.

Also, Apple has lavished an unprecedented level of attention on the iPhone 11 's Pro video capabilities, making the iPhone one of the best that can be compared to some DSLR. Unlike many other competing flagships able to deliver high frame rates and quality picture resolution from the phone's primary camera, the iPhone 11 Pro and Pro Max can capture 4K-resolution video at 60 frames per second from any of its rear lenses effortlessly with high quality. The good thing is, you can easily change any of those settings.

Even when you are taking a picture with one of your cameras, your iPhone is assisting with the overall exposure levels and white balance with the other two camera sensors in the background, hence the perspective transition is seamless, and your image details preserved.

One More Thing

Thank you so much for spending time reading this book.

If you have enjoyed reading this book as much as I have enjoyed writing it, I'd appreciate if you could post a kind review in the comment's section. It does help to motivate me, knowing that I have been able to help someone with a little of my effort.

However, if you have comments on possible areas that need improvement or want to make a recommendation or you have something you specifically want us to include that wasn't captured in this edition, you can contact me here or send mail to linda.shift1@gmail.com and I will do my best to address it.

Thanks once again for taking your time to read this book.

Don't Forget to Join Our Fans' Page and Let's get to talk more or search for Awesome Book Collections on Facebook.

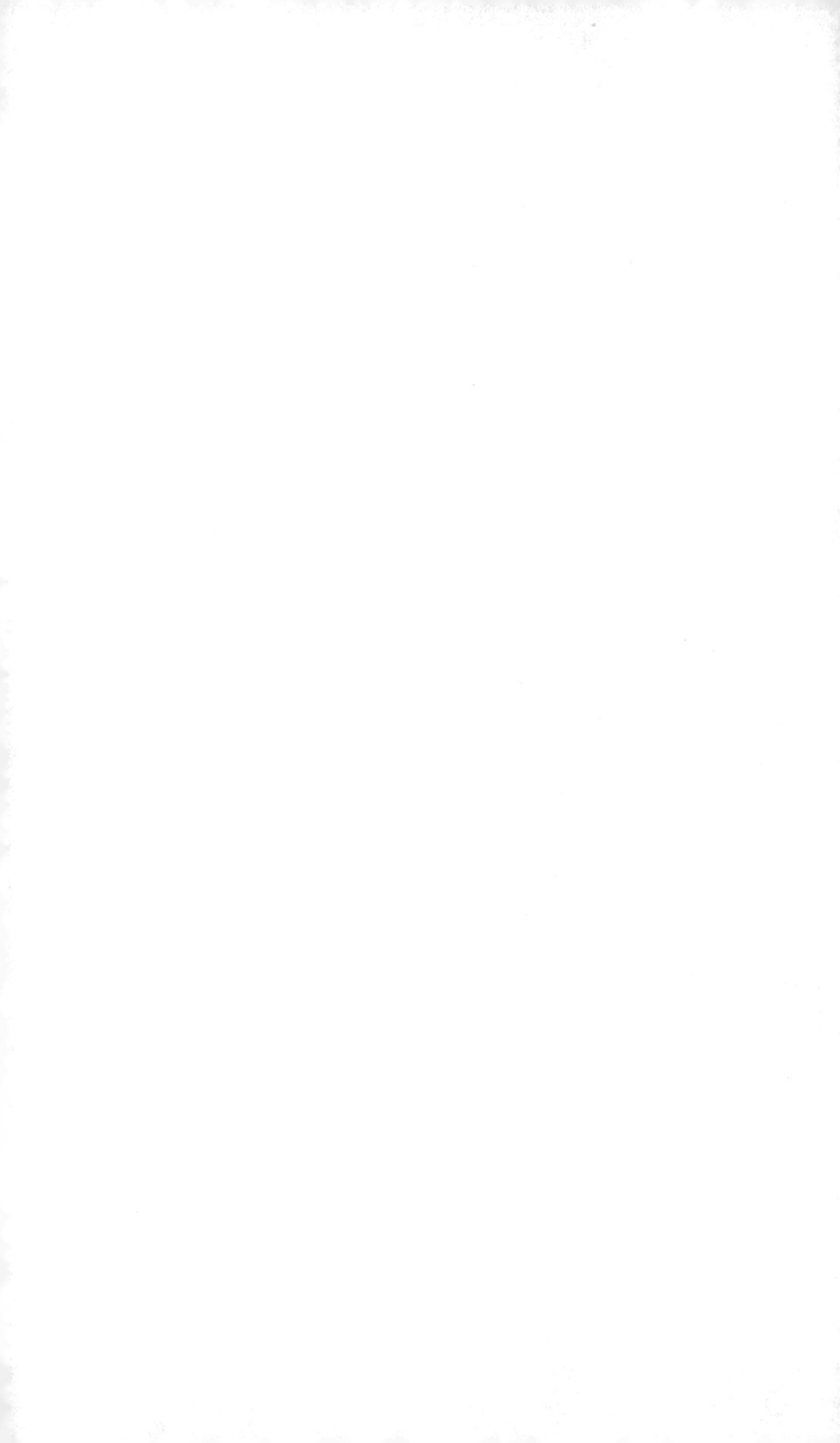